Inner Voices, Inner Views

Conversations with Southern Writers

Inner Voices, Inner Views

Conversations with Southern Writers

by Pam Kingsbury

The Enolam Group, Inc.

The interviews in this book, with the exceptions of H. E. Francis
(which first appeared in *FirstDraft,* the journal of the Alabama Writers'
Forum, in the spring 2005 issue), and Mary Ward Brown, were
published first in *Southern Scribe.* Some interviews have been slightly
modified for this publication.

This project has been made possible for the author by a partnership
that includes the National Endowment for the Arts and the Alabama
State Council on the Arts.

Thank you to the following people: the writers who, in addition to
providing many hours of excellent reading, gave so freely of their time
and themselves in discussing their work; Jay Lamar and Joyce Dixon
for permissions; the publisher for suggesting the title; Shannon Wells
for the cover photographs; Anita Miller Garner and Lisa Graves Minor
for proofreading; and Cindy McDonald for her assistance.

ISBN: 09715536-4-5

LCCN: 2005930608

Table of contents

for Jack

Introduction

Think of the last great book you read. What wouldn't you pay to be able to talk to the writer about motives, influences, characters, work habits, motifs, the way to become a writer, the way to write?

Books and the people who write them are fascinating, plain and simple. They have something. It may be a vision or insight, but certainly it is a gift for offering us a take on things that enrich or teach, that take us outside ourselves, or reveal us to ourselves. The "itch to know" what something is and how something happens is powerful.

Who are these people? Where are they from? What books do they read? What advice can they give to those of us who aspire to be like them?

If we can't ask our questions directly, may we at least be lucky enough to find the record of someone who has. You have it here.

Through thoughtful questions formed by knowledge of writers and their works, this book brings us the authors' views on their best work, on their influences, on how they found a character's voice, on book signings and critics, on where inspiration comes from and how to cope when it sometimes disappears, on what an author wishes someone would ask, and on what the writer hopes is never asked again.

It is fitting that the intimate art of writing is probed through the give and take of an interview. Good questions get rich, surprising, often revealing answers. And it turns out that writers like to talk. They are generous, thoughtful partners in the process of inquiry. It gives them a chance, as one writer said, to talk about "how lives get shaped, how fate interferes with plans—all that good stuff."

So these interviews are true dialogues. And we get to be a part of that. What could be better?

Jay Lamar—Auburn Center for the Arts and Humanities
The Alabama Center for the Book

Rick Bragg

Had his family not produced "a writer guy," Rick Bragg's family stories—of his mother's sacrifice for her children, of his larger-than-life grandfather, and the disappearing blue-collar culture of the foothills of the Appalachian Mountains—might have been lost.

Bragg, who grew up just outside of Jacksonville, Alabama, won a Pulitzer Prize for his work at the *New York Times*. The judges praised Bragg for his "elegantly written stories on contemporary America." He's won more than forty journalism awards, spent a year at Harvard on a Neiman Fellowship, and has written three bestsellers.

"Touched in a personal rather than a professional way," Bragg has had an outpouring of thanks from people all over the country thanking him for giving "poor people" a voice in literature.

Every interview with you has to start with the question— how is your mother?

(Laughter.) She's doing pretty good. She's becoming ornery and obstinate in her old age. *All Over But the Shoutin'* was written specifically to honor her, which made her a little uncomfortable. Being called the finest momma on earth embarrasses her.

How did *Ava's Man* come to be?

At every book signing, it seemed like 1,000 little old ladies told me I'd left out the good part. And when so many readers— people are smart down here—were telling me that, I thought I might ought to listen.

I was talking with my editor about writing a book about the disappearing of the blue-collar workers in the South, which are as much an endangered species as anything in the rain forest. I wanted to write about the homogenization of the Deep South. She suggested I find a way to tell it with only one person and capture time.

The only man I wanted to tell a story about died a few months before I was born—my grandfather Charlie Bundrum. I wasn't sure I could do it until I started talking with my kinfolks.

Ava's Man was much more fun to write than *All Over But the Shoutin'* because it didn't have the unremitting sadness.

It seems like every time my family would start to talk about Charlie, my grandmother (Ava) would not be denied. She intruded on every memory.

Forty-three years later, Charlie's children still cry when they say his name. Now, I guarantee you, no one will cry for me like that when I'm gone. The way they miss him is extraordinary and I thought a man like that deserved a book.

Writing *Ava's Man* was much more fun for the family; at sixty-five and seventy, they've enjoyed telling the stories.

Was your extended family (aunts, uncles, and cousins) happy with the memoir?

I gave the manuscript to my mother, aunts, sister-in-law Teresa, and cousin Jackie, with crossed fingers because I knew if I ever let his wings drag in the dust, his surviving daughters would have done more than forget my birthday. If they had not approved of the book it would have never seen the light of day.

Talk about the difference between writing *Shoutin'* and *Ava's Man.*

Writing *Ava's Man* was ten times easier than writing *Shoutin'* and I had more fun doing it.

Shoutin' is three books cobbled together. It's the story of my mother's sacrifices, our childhood, and my career in journalism. I wanted to show what my momma had won and the sadness that shaped our family.

Ava's Man took two years to write. I got to build me a grandfather and what's better than that?

I hope *Ava's Man* is a complete story of a life and time— the first fifty years of the last century and how a man could slay the dragon of poverty. I got to write about people who aren't usually written about in fiction.

Ava's Man dovetails neatly. Hopefully, it answers the question, "Why did my mother marry my father?" and will satisfy the readers who insisted we do it. There's nothing better on the planet than a book signing or seeing people in the airport who smile and keep walking while telling me, "I read your book."

Which book is closer to your heart?

Shoutin' will always be the book I'm most proud of and affected by because it is a story for people who love their mothers. My mother *really* did go eighteen years without a new dress so her sons could have more.

Would you like to see movies made from either of your memoirs?

We're (the Bragg family) uncomfortable with making a movie from *Shoutin'* because it's still too deeply personal to the living.

I think about my grandfather's image and the tough actors seem weak. I laugh out loud thinking about an actor drinking imported mineral water with a twist of lime and then playing Charlie beating the hell of the state troopers.

You've won a Pulitzer Prize, your newspaper work has been anthologized (*Somebody Told Me*), you've written three bestsellers, garnered both critical and popular acclaim, and been nominated for a Grammy. What do you still want to do?

In *Ava's Man*, I hint at writing about the generations beyond me, what it means to be a blue-collar Southerner.

When I moved to New Orleans, people said, "Oh, you'll write about New Orleans now." No, I'm not an expert on New Orleans. I'm not an expert on anything. But I know the foothills of the Appalachians and I don't have to elbow anybody out of the way to write about the people who walked out of the cotton fields, put down their cotton sacks, and went into the mills that ate them alive. If I have a mission, it's to write about their strength of character.

Hootie, Jesse Clines, the simple-minded man Charlie adopted, has always fascinated me. There were some great stories about him. He almost never spoke but I keep thinking, "What if all the lies told him were the truth?" So little is known, I'd like to write about him in fiction and bridge the genres.

After seven years of being interviewed, what would you still like to be asked?

My favorite question came from Scottie Vickery at the *Birmingham News*. She asked my momma about the best day of her life. (And my momma is still uncomfortable with being interviewed.)

I hoped maybe she'd say, "The day my boy wrote the book about me, or the day my boy won the Pulitzer Prize, or the day my boy gave me the keys to my house," but she actually told her about (dramatic pause), "The birth of my *first* son."

(Laughter.) Books and houses are just paper and wood to her. What matters is her sons.

I always ask the question now and I like thinking about the best hour and the best day. It's my favorite question to think about.

Selected bibliography of Rick Bragg

Non-fiction:

All Over But the Shoutin'
Somebody Told Me: The Newspaper Stories of Rick Bragg
Redbirds: Memories from the South (the United Kingdom version of *Shoutin'*)
Ava's Man
I Am A Soldier, Too: The Jessica Lynch Story

Larry Brown

1951 – 2004

From the 1988 publication of his first collection of short stories, *Facing the Music*, through the publication of the last novel published in the author's lifetime, *The Rabbit Factory*, Larry Brown's work was praised for portraying poor, hard-working, and even harder-living Southerners with honesty.

Larry Brown, who lived outside of Oxford, Mississippi, in the Tula community, remained true to his upbringing. Like his father, he served in the military, and like the characters in his fiction, Brown worked at a variety of jobs before settling into a job as a full-time firefighter, a position he held from 1973 until 1990.

A self-taught writer, Brown always said he learned to write by being an avid reader. Pat Conroy and Barry Hannah were early champions of his work. Winner of two Southern Book Critics Awards for Fiction and the Lila Wallace Reader's Digest Writer's Award, Brown's work was often compared to Faulkner's.

Brown's novel *Big Bad Love* was made into a movie starring Debra Winger and directed by Arliss Howard. Gary Hawkins's documentary, *The Rough South of Larry Brown*, seems destined to be the best commentary on Larry Brown's life and work. It's hard to imagine contemporary Southern literature without the influence of Larry Brown. His books have been eagerly anticipated, widely read, and praised by critics. His characters reflect the raw elements of the South, where they need "grit" to survive.

Which character or image from *The Rabbit Factory* came to you first?

Arthur was the first character who came to me. It was just an image of an old guy trying to catch a wild kitten in a cage trap. That first paragraph was written in 1994, and the following six or seven chapters, and then I laid it aside since it was getting bigger than a short story, which was what I originally intended.

Why did you change publishers?

I was with Algonquin for eight books and fourteen years. I think they tried very hard to market my books, and I did win a lot of prizes. This book was something different, something of a departure, I guess, and I had to go elsewhere.

Each of your books has been radically different from its predecessor. Have you ever felt forced to write for the marketplace?

I don't really worry about what politically correct people are going to think about my books. I'm not writing the books for them. I'm writing them for the person who likes to read fiction about people they can relate to, not judge, but maybe understand and have a little compassion for.

As far as writing what you want to, in the midst of all the politically correct bullshit, it's imperative. I've always felt that people ought to talk (I'm talking about characters in fiction), the way they really would depending on where they live, because geography shapes language and the lives of the people who live there. Your concern should be creating a real world on paper. To do that, it has to have authenticity to the time and place, and it has to reveal the many intricacies of the human heart, which is sometimes twisted and bent. The main thing you have to do is tell a good story. That's all there is. Anything less sucks.

At one time you sponsored a reading series in Oxford. How did it come about and are you still involved?

No, the readers series I had going has been over for almost two years now. I was living on a Lila Wallace-Readers Digest Award that gave me a very generous $35,000 per year for three years and also provided $10,000 per year to finance the program I chose, which was to bring in writers from all over the country to give readings and writing workshops at our local library. It was a great opportunity to get a lot of my friends down here for a weekend while exposing local readers to fine writers they might not have encountered before. It also allowed me to live and write mostly unmolested for three years. Priceless.

Do you want to discuss living in Oxford?

The Oxford connection. Well. It gets asked about a lot. I don't get up there much because I'm usually working in here every night. I don't really have much time to get out and see friends the way I wish I could and still get my work done. It's not good for me to go to a bar and drink. I'll stay all night, have one hell of a good time, and feel bad the next day. I used to hang out all the time. And sometimes days stretched into months. This always accompanied lots of guitar playing, which earns nothing and is only entertainment, or diversion, or a means of not working, like drinking. I've found after all these years that I can't drink and write at the same time, so most of the time I choose writing.

There weren't many young writers in Oxford when I was coming up. I think there are a lot of them now. Lots of young people come up and introduce themselves, and say they appreciate my work, and that's always nice to hear. It's a good thing for young people to like what you do.

William Faulkner, John Grisham, Barry Hannah. All of them in Oxford. John not so much any more. I just happened to be born here and loved to read. There are more writers coming here all the time to live and write, some of them established. The bookstore, Square Books, draws thousands of people. It's one reason Oxford is such a popular place for writers and readers. Jim Harrison loves it here, loves the food. Arliss Howard and Debra Winger shot *Big Bad Love* here. It's getting to be a very popular place to move to. It's weird seeing what it's like now, the square full of bars and restaurants, and remembering what it was like back in the fifties and sixties when I was a kid and there was absolutely nothing going on at night. It's a whole new world. And sometimes it's hard for me to move around in it. But that just goes along with what I do with my life. Most of the time I stay out here in the country and write. And work on my shack. And feed my catfish.

Which writers do you consider your literary influences?

Flannery O'Connor, Charles Bukowski, Raymond Carver, William Faulkner, Cormac McCarthy, and Harry Crews.

Who are some of the younger writers readers should be reading?

Silas House. Nancy Jean Peacock. June Spence. Brad Watson's got two wonderful books. Daniel Wallace. George Singleton's good. It's hard to keep up with everybody. I get a lot of books here from publishers wanting blurbs, and I just can't read them all. I'll be interested to see what Charles Frazier does next. John DuFrense. There's a lot of good writers out there. It's hard to come up with a list because you'll surely leave somebody good out.

Do you have any advice for aspiring authors?

Rejection.
Trial and error.
Make lots of stupid mistakes.
There are no shortcuts.
You have to learn to write fiction that grabs the reader by the throat and doesn't let him go until you're through with him.

And the only way to do that is to sit down and spend years writing and failing and writing again.

If you quit, nobody's ever going to hear from you.

Are there any questions you're tired of being asked?

Gee, I've been asked the same ones so many times it's hard to remember. A lady interviewed me for some tape recordings one time and she had good questions about *Joe*. I was able to sit there and talk not only about him, but about the environment and what happens to the woods when big timber companies cut hardwoods down and replant with pines, and how the animals all have to leave, because there's nothing for them to eat if the oaks and acorns they produce are gone. I was able to talk about the evolution of the landscape around here I've seen since I was eighteen and how much it's changed. How Faulkner foretold it. How lives get shaped. How fate interferes with plans...all that good stuff.

What's the one question you've always wanted to be asked?

I can't think of anything I'm waiting to be asked. I just try to give a little encouragement to young writers without taking them personally under my wing, although I have taken more than a few and tucked them under there already. But I try to do it in a way that gives them a realistic view of what they're facing if they want to be fiction writers. It is not easy, and I've seen people quit their jobs over it, then fail. I didn't quit my job until I'd published some books and had some more writing gigs lined up. And I failed plenty before than. Five novels. Burned one. I've written about 150 short stories. Poetry. All bad. I've done a ton of non-fiction, and love writing it. There are boxes and boxes and boxes of unpublished stuff in my attic. That's what it takes—boxes and boxes of stuff that's no good for anything. But you have to sit there and write it anyway to learn how to do it right. That's the rules. No way around it if you want to be a really good writer.

What do you enjoy most about your book tours?

It's real good to see people who have read your books again and again in other cities. You look forward to eating in favorite restaurants in Seattle, and giving a reading at Elliott Bay or A Clean, Well-Lighted Place. There's no telling who may show up. I've got friends all over and it's good to see them. It's nice to be able to go to L.A. and stay with a friend at his house. I hear from people all over this country, and they turn out when you hit their town. It's a wide world with lot of good people in it. Independent bookstores have supported me, and I worry about their future. They will hand-sell a book they like, and that's how good books get on the bestseller list, by sheer weight of numbers sold. A book that is too good to ignore. But it doesn't happen to every good book. It even happens to bad books. But that's just the world. You can't have everything perfect.

Would you like to write another book of non-fiction?

Sure, I'd love to write about the little house I've been building for five years by myself, and the eight acres of woods and pasture land it sits on, and the birds and animals that live there, and the fish I raise and catch in my pond, and all the work I do over there with a tractor and chainsaw and a log chain and shovel, but non-fiction doesn't sell nearly as well as novels, so I'll probably just keep writing novels.

I plan to write some original screenplays. Right now, I'm writing my third screenplay. This one is about the life of Hank Williams.

I also have two novels in progress. My new publisher likes them. This is good.

Selected bibliography of Larry Brown

Fiction:

Big Bad Love
Father and Son
Joe
Fay
Facing the Music
The Rabbit Factory
Dirty Work

Non-fiction:

Billy Ray's Farm
On Fire

Mary Ward Brown

Mary Ward Brown deals with life—and writing—with equanimity. When asked about her stories, she's quick to point out the hard work—and rewriting—in every sentence of every story she's ever written.

Her first collection, *Tongues of Flame* (published in 1986), was the 1987 winner of the Pen/Hemingway Award, the 1987 Alabama Library Association Award, and the 1991 Lillian Smith Award.

It Wasn't All Dancing, published in 2002, garnered excellent reviews and a *ForeWord* Book of the Year Award. Mrs. Brown was the winner of the 2002 Harper Lee Award for Distinguished Alabama Writer and the 2003 Hillsdale Prize in Fiction.

Let's talk about your childhood home.

My "so-called" childhood home was built by my father in the early '20s. It was next door to his store, in a farming community called Hamburg. He had a sawmill as part of his farm operation, and when the timber was cut he saved some of the heart pine lumber to build this house. They (my parents) picked a house plan from a book, and—I still have that book. The style of architecture is not beautiful, but the heart pine was, and that makes the house less ordinary.

You raised a son in this house...

My son was not born here. I married the publicity director of Auburn University, [which was then] called Alabama Polytechnic Institute. We lived in Auburn for seven years, and my son was born there in the Drake Infirmary. When my father died

I inherited part of the farm, so we moved back here when he was four years old.

Did you know you wanted to be a writer when you were growing up on the farm?

Oh, I didn't think of it in those terms. I didn't know any writers. We weren't a bookish family and there were no books around. But I always liked words and liked to make sentences. It was a natural thing.

When I went to high school, I was interested in journalism, and editor of the paper for two years. Then when I went to Judson, the same thing happened.

I never had a creative writing teacher in those years. But they did have a good journalism teacher at Judson—Mae Brunson was her name. So I took journalism and loved it, and I'm glad I did, because it's great training for any writer, I think.

I just wanted to write stories. I don't know why. Maybe the same instinct as "Kilroy was here." I've always been glad to be alive, and I've thought about the things I see and hear. A lot of it is wonderful and I wanted to preserve a little of it, I guess. Things that are tragic are as valuable as those that are good. I mean, whatever's human is good material if you tell the truth about it. I like whatever's genuine in people and in art. So I just wanted to tell the truth—good or bad. I think it has a better chance of enduring, the truth does.

Do you have any suggestions for young writers?

I think you have to really want to write if you want to be published. You have to realize that it's hard work. At least, it has been for me. For some writers the work seems to come easily, but it didn't for me. I just go sentence by sentence. There's also technique to writing fiction and writers need to know it. Some can be absorbed through reading, and a lot from trial and error. Creative writing classes sometime help. They helped me, one at the University of Alabama, another by correspondence from the University of North Carolina. It's also good to find people who will help you. People who know what's good and what's not, who will read what you've written and tell you honestly what they think. What you need is criticism, not praise.

Who were some of the writers who influenced your work?

Many people have asked that question. I've always loved the short story form. The first two short story writers I really loved were Katherine Mansfield and Katherine Ann Porter. In time, I thought Katherine Mansfield was a little "precious," but the Katherine Ann Porter stories still hold up for me.

In college I was always working on school papers and never had time to read...But when I married (on my twenty-second birthday) and went to Auburn with my husband, they had a wonderful library and I read down the Thomas Wolfe shelf. Later I read Chekhov and Tolstoy and would hate to have to choose between them. Russian writers deal with the human experience more faithfully than most, I think. We have Faulkner and Melville, Flannery O'Conner. But overall, next to the Southern writers, I love Russian writers more than any.

Do you think it's harder for women to carve out time for their own work?

For women of my generation, certainly.

Tillie Olsen wrote wonderful short stories, but not many. They came out in a collection called *Tell Me a Riddle*. But she was married, had children, and not much money. So she had to work and help out. She didn't have the energy for both, so she gave up on fiction. She did get together a book called *Silences*, which documented the struggle of women with families who wanted to be writers. It's an interesting book.

I don't know about women of this generation. Their choices seem to be less cut-and-dried. There are now good women writers with families and children. I don't know how their children will turn out.

**Let's talk about your first collection of short stories,
Tongues of Flame. Your first book was published when
many people are winding down their careers.**

Wasn't I seventy? That was 1986. (Chuckling) Well...it
was a great surprise to me and I'm sure to many others.

In the '50s, while my son Kirtley was young, I wrote
stories while he was in school. Some of them were published in
the quarterlies. But I was so torn all the time. My husband had
given up a good job at Auburn to come over here and run a farm
I had inherited. We were having a hard time, and here I was, shut
up in a room upstairs writing fiction that didn't sell. My
conscience hurt so much I decided I'd have to give it up, and did
for twenty-five years.

In 1970, when my husband died, a year went by before I
could even read fiction. Fiction didn't seem important. Also, I
had to learn to do all the things he'd always done, like run the
place, pay the bills, before I could do anything else.

When I finally got myself together, I found that I'd
learned a little about writing fiction in the past. I'd first tried to
write stories back in Auburn. I'd start but couldn't bring them
together, didn't have the technique to finish. But since then, I'd
studied writing in the two creative writing courses, and had had
stories in the quarterlies. So now, since I had time, I thought I'd
try again. My friends told me I shouldn't be doing it, that I should
be out in the world, not shut up in the country trying to write
fiction.

I didn't get anything published for several years. One day
when I went to town, a woman said to me, "Are you STILL out
there trying to write?"

When "The Amaryllis" was finally published in McCall's,
everyone was carried away with it, because they said it didn't have
sex or violence. And after that, people seemed to give me the
right to write.

So I worked as hard as I could for ten years, and those
were wonderful writing years. I didn't have so many
interruptions. I'd get up at 4:30 in the morning, passionate to get

started. I'd work as long as I could concentrate, then get the mail, tend to a few things, fix a lunch, and work some more.

I had long, free days with uninterrupted time. That's how the stories for *Tongues of Flame* got written. The book's success was a complete surprise to me, to everybody. I was not aiming for any kind of success. I was just trying to write the stories. It wasn't even my idea to write a book.

You were invited to Russia as a result of the publication of *Tongues of Flame*. Would you like to talk about the experience?

Seymour Lawrence, who was a literary publisher at Dutton, published my first book. Later he moved from Dutton to Houghton Mifflin. Sometime after that, "The Cure," my story about an old black woman and an old white doctor, was selected for inclusion in *The Human Experience*, an anthology of writing by American and Russian writers. It was put together by a group of Quakers and edited by William Styron. Because my publisher had moved, the letter saying my story had been selected took a while to find me. It was already late to respond, but I called up at once and accepted. Soon I got a call from one of the organizers. She said she hoped I wouldn't be offended if she asked me a question. "Are you white or are you black?" she said.

The two groups of writers met first in Washington D.C., and spent five days together. We got to know the Russian writers and were carried away with them. We (the American writers) couldn't speak their language but we managed to communicate. When they (the Russian writers) wanted to tell us they liked something, for instance, they'd pat themselves over the heart. In the meetings, of course, there were translators.

A year later, the Soviet Writers' Union invited those of us in the book to come to Russia. We were to pay our own air fare but be guests of the Writers' Union once we were there.

This was during the time of Perestroika. The Writer's Union was politically powerful and some of the writers we'd met in Washington were not in it, and not there to meet us. But we were royally treated, with private rooms in a fine hotel, wonderful food, and trips to literary sites, mainly Pushkin's. Our old friends did come to see us while we were there.

I had always loved the Russian writers.

What did you see that surprised you?

I was not surprised, really. Moscow was beautiful. The people were warm and hospitable and I liked them, felt at home there.

I wanted to see Chekhov's house and the estate where the Tolstoy marriage played itself out. One day Joyce Johnson, Sharon Olds, and I walked to Chekhov's house in Moscow. Before we went in we were supposed to slip our shoes into big slides, but we took off our shoes altogether. We felt we were entering a shrine. There was a room of Chekhov memorabilia and I saw his little wire-rimmed glasses. Tears came into my eyes when I saw those little glasses. It was wonderful to go there.

I remember saying that they (the Russians) have suffered and so have Southerners. Slavery, lost war, reconstruction, racial upheaval, always rebuilding from something. Losers but survivors, so far, and by the hardiest. Gives depth to both literatures.

The only American writer in evidence in Russia was Faulkner. His books were everywhere.

I loved the people, the hotel maids, taxi drivers, old war veterans, men and women, still wearing their medals. Poor, but quick to smile at us. They're also a brave people. Hitler went over there, and they were the ones who broke his back. When we were there the stores were poorly stocked and people had to stand in line for bread and meat.

When we rode on the bus through the countryside, we saw these little houses painted beautiful colors, subtle mixed colors, with fancy grillwork. They were darling little houses and we wanted to see what they were like inside. The bus driver stopped and our guide asked one owner if we could come in. The first one declined, but at the second house they invited us in. The house was set on a slope and the cows were kept under the house. The farmer had about an acre. The bed wasn't made, because the woman was off at her job, and the kitchen was primitive. The stove looked homemade. The furnishings were so meager and the family so cordial, it broke my heart. When we got back on the bus, I started to cry. I'd suddenly realized that that's how people from other sections of the country feel when they come to Alabama…

There was a long gap between the publications of your two collections of short stories (*Tongues of Flame* and *It Wasn't All Dancing*).

It took longer the second time. There was so much else to do. By then, I'd met other writers and had literary obligations. I still had the same family ties and had to keep the house and farm going.

It takes time and strength, physical strength, to write, and I could no longer get up at 4:30 in the morning to work.

What's been the highlight of the writing life for you?

I don't know. I can't think of any one thing that stands above everything. There have been so many good things.

I can think of one bad thing. There was a review of *Tongues of Flame* by Jonathan Yardley in the *Washington Post*. He said that I "was well-intentioned but not subtle, and hadn't found my voice." He went on and on. I saved that one. Every now and then, when I get a little praise, I read it and think, "who knows, who knows?"

What's the best day of your life?

The very best day? I think that's the day my son was born. No experience has ever compared to seeing that child I brought into this world.

What have you never been asked by an interviewer that you'd still like to be asked?

(Laughter) I'm always braced for the next question. I'm afraid I'll be blindsided.

Selected bibliography of Mary Ward Brown

Fiction:

Tongues of Flame
It Wasn't All Dancing

Kelly Cherry

Kelly Cherry's resume reads like a Who's Who in contemporary American literature. She's published seven works of fiction (most recently *We Can Still be Friends*), two memoirs, six collections of poetry, seven chapbooks, two translations of classical drama, and a collection of "prose about poetry," *History, Passion, Freedom, Death, and Hope.* Even after publishing almost thirty works, she modestly hopes "What I'm doing is original. I hope that I write in a voice with new ways to say what I've always wanted to say."

Do you feel that you are a Southern writer? Southerner?

I'm certainly a Southerner. Even though I've lived out of the South—England, New York, the Midwest, and elsewhere— my heritage is Southern and I've never not felt Southern. I'm also a writer who writes in and sometimes about the South. I don't mind being called a Southern writer—indeed, I enjoy the collegiality of it and admire the way Southern readers cherish and continue the tradition of literature about the South—although I think the term may be misleading if it suggests that I'm a regional writer. I've written too much set elsewhere to be considered regional, and my early cultural influences were not Southern.

What are those cultural influences?

The ancients, especially Catullus and Sophocles. Shakespeare, who is every writer's greatest influence. The Bible writers, who are the greatest influence on every writer in the South. The Russians, with whom I fell in love very early on. Thomas Hardy and Thomas Mann. Joyce may have been a bigger influence than I used to recognize him for. Yeats, Stevens, T. S. Eliot, Frost. Philosophers.

And I read a great many plays in high school and college.

Those are the writers I grew up on. We didn't have many children's books in the house—they weren't yet being mass-marketed in paperback, and in any case, my parents felt it was foolish to spend money on books when they could be checked out from a library. But I have vivid memories of *The Poky Little Puppy*, *The Little Train That Could*, *Babar the Elephant*, and *The Ugly Duckling*.

What are you currently working on?

I always work on several books at once. I spend time on one thing, move to another, move to yet another, go back to the first: this lets me spend more conceptual time with each thing than I would have otherwise. Currently well underway are a couple of collections of poems, a collection of essays about women fiction writers and about being a woman who writes fiction, a memoir, and a group of stories set in the South. Not every book one writes finds a publisher, of course, and so I can't say that all of these projects will find their way to bookshelves.

Your husband, Burke Davis III, is also a fiction writer (*Dwelling Places*). What is it like living in the house with another writer?

Burke and I talk about ideas for stories and books and read each other's work. He is a marvelous fiction writer and I almost always take his suggestions for revision of my fiction.

What are the nuts and bolts of writing for you?

I write in longhand. At some point I move to a typewriter or, these days, a computer, but my first drafts are always longhand and I often revert to longhand in later stages when I'm working out a difficult passage or scene. I don't have a set time for writing; I just squeeze it in whenever I can. For me, poetry requires more time than fiction. Once a story or, especially, a novel is begun, there is a narrative thread one can pick up in a spare moment, but poetry demands silence and space, freedom from worry, a concentration that can leave you wrung out and exhausted.

What is your best advice to beginning writers?

Read, write, know tools and techniques, and make good friends who share your passion and will stick by you.

What do you think is at the heart of your work?

From an early age, from even before I understood that books were written by people and not simply things that appeared *sui generis*, and even before I had words to say it with, I had something to say. It is something that cannot be talked about; it can only be demonstrated, which, of course, is why one turns to art rather than to philosophy, as I might have done. This need to say what was mine to say preceded anything else in my life. I think it was my earliest response to life and was a response to what Beethoven made me feel, and who knows, since my parents were playing Beethoven while I was still in the womb, maybe this need even preceded my own life. That's how it has always felt, anyway.

Is any of your work autobiographical?

All serious fiction begins in autobiography, though the connection may remain hidden from the reader. Serious fiction is, however, fiction; it proceeds from the real to the imagined. Often, the better imagined a fiction is, the more likely it is that a reader will mistake it for autobiography.

Readers—among them, other writers—have asked me what arrangements I make for my daughter when I travel to give readings (*The Society of Friends*); why I went to med school if I'm not practicing (*Sick and Full of Burning*); if they can tell me about their own recollections of my ex-husband's father (*Augusta Played*); if I enjoyed my time in Bolivia (*In the Wink of an Eye*). No daughter. Couldn't cut up a frog, much less a person. Never met my ex-husband's father. Have never been to Bolivia.

I have written one autobiography, *The Exiled Heart*, and some personal essays, a form that makes use of the materials of autobiography and memoir.

Selected bibliography of Kelly Cherry

Fiction:

The Society of Friends
My Life and Dr. Joyce Brothers
The Lost Traveller's Dream
In the Wink of an Eye
Augusta Played
Sick and Full of Burning
We Can Still Be Friends

Poetry:

Rising Venus
Death and Transfiguration
God's Loud Hand
Natural Theology
Relativity
Lovers and Agnostics

Non-fiction:

Writing the World
The Exiled Heart
History, Passion, Freedom, Death, and Hope: Prose about Poetry

Patricia Foster

Patricia Foster's works are about women's lives—what it means to be identified by gender, race, place, and socio-economic class. Using the everyday to define her life—her roles as daughter, sister, wife, college professor, writer—she writes about the changes she's seen during her lifetime.

A professor in the MFA Program in Nonfiction at the University of Iowa, she is the author of *All the Lost Girls* and *Just Beneath My Skin,* editor of *Minding the Body: Women Writers on Body and Soul* and *Sister to Sister,* and the co-editor of *The Healing Circle.*

Introduce yourself.

I grew up in a little town in Southern Alabama where my father was a doctor and my mother a science teacher. After graduating from public schools, I went to Vanderbilt University and then to UCLA where I got an MFA in art. I fell in love with photography and video at UCLA, but it was on a camping trip after I finished my MFA that I realized I liked 'writing' the scenes for the video more than actually filming them. It was a kind of 'wake-up' call, a vital moment that surprised me. I moved to Seattle, began taking writing classes, and then raced across the country to get my MFA in creative writing at the Iowa Writers' Workshop. It felt like a race, an urgent sense that I had to catch up with myself and let the stories out. I say this because when I left the South I felt lost to myself and by telling stories, I began to feel 'found.'

Most of your work is non-fiction—arguably an unusual choice for a Southern writer—do you see a need for good essayists in Southern literature?

Not long ago I was browsing in an independent bookstore in a Southern city. There was a huge section labeled 'Southern Fiction' and a history section labeled 'Southern Non-fiction.' I saw such prominent books as *Carry Me Home* (Diane McWhorter) and *The Liar's Club* (Mary Karr), but I saw no books of essays, no collected works of non-fiction. Why, I asked myself, is there no Joan Didion, no James Baldwin, no Vivian Gornick among Southern writers?

My answer is a complicated one, and yet my first instinct is perhaps the most reliable. I believe you have to teach a culture how to read a genre just as you teach a culture how to read itself. It's an act of self-assessment, an act of assertion. It's a process of awakening. It requires that the literary essay and the memoir be placed in a context, given a narrative reference point in much the same way that contemporary poetry has begun to do. A story drops you into a dramatic moment and builds on that drama, making you wonder: What will happen next? How will this resolve itself? The essay often uses dramatic narrative as well, but it also depends on the reflective lens, the willingness of the writer to meditate on a moment or an event or an issue and bring you to a sense of closure through analysis rather than drama.

In the 1990s, autobiographical writing was catapulted into a post-modern context, giving birth to the Personal History column in *The New Yorker*, to regular essay features in such magazines as *Harper's, The Atlantic Monthly, The Oxford American*, and *Salon*. What I think the memoir and the personal essay offered was a return to intimacy, a sense of reflection and meditation about cultural and personal identity. As Joan Didion once said, "We live entirely by the imposition of a narrative line upon disparate images." In America during the last decade that narrative line has fashioned itself in autobiography and the personal essay with the writer's need to locate the self in a transient world—not just the political world of the 20th century but the world of personal identity in conflict with constant change.

Just Beneath My Skin is subtitled _Autobiography and Self-Discovery_. What was your most surprising discovery during the writing of these essays?

What comes to mind are two things: First, that I can love something deeply, feel that it's inside me, 'in my bones,' and simultaneously not like it very much. For example, I love Fairhope, Alabama, the town where I was born, the place that was my intellectual mentor, my creative guide. I love its beauty and its grace and its original political intent to neutralize the caste system that has so often marred Southern culture. I loved its narrow lanes, the back pastures where I rode horses, its emphasis on a liberal spirit of education. Each time I went to my music lesson at Mama Dot's, I imagined that here was a place where ideas got a fair shake, where dissent was spoken, where creative life was not only approved but desired. But when I came back after years in other parts of the country, it had changed, been hijacked by the moneyed class, become commercialized and conservative. I still love Fairhope—and there are many writers there I enjoy reading—but I don't like it very much right now. And I had to write about that in "The New Royalists" because it was something I needed to sort out in myself.

Second, I discovered that I could step outside of myself, out of my comfort zone. I went to Tuskegee, Alabama, not knowing what I'd find, even what I was looking for. I went, just as James Agee went to live with sharecroppers during the Depression, to understand something about humanity that I couldn't know by staying in my middle-class life in Iowa City, Iowa. I think we all want immunity from problems, but when that immunity makes you myopic to the real concerns that exist every day for other people, self-protection becomes blindness.

Which of your essays has been the most difficult to write and discuss?

What was the most difficult to write was "Outside the Hive," the essay about why I've remained childless. In writing it, I was obsessed with the psychological and sociological reasons for why I had never had children, why 'giving birth to voice' was more important to me than 'giving birth to a child' in my youth (and childbearing years). If I'm honest, I wish I'd had the chance for both. I wish I could have successfully overcome my insecurities and been both a mother and a writer. It just took me a long time to 'grow myself up.' If I were 35 right now, I'm sure I'd have children.

I came of age in the turbulent '60s and though I was no fire-breathing radical, I was deeply affected by the issues the country confronted: civil rights and women's rights particularly. I think many of us gain a political education through crisis and the '60s provided that, a deep division between the institutionalized power of the status quo and the marginalized power of those who questioned the morality of segregation, the subordination of women and the concerns of the Vietnam War. Because courageous people put their lives on the line, the status quo changed. Equality took a step forward. At least in terms of a human being's rights before the law. Economic and social equality are another thing entirely and what frightens me now is that we're becoming more deeply divided by the economic realities of the 21st century, the sense of an entitled class— wealthy and dominant and secure—and an underclass—under-educated, under-employed and dependent. I see many people who believe the American Dream can still be accomplished by hard work and loyalty, but, on the whole, I think that's naïve. We have a wide disparity in our educational systems, a wide disparity in our income levels, a wide disparity in our health care. The truth is that lack of preparation often cannot be overcome by hard work alone. What I hope is that we begin to revise public education so that a child's mental landscape is not governed by the economic base of his/her geography.

Does living in the Midwest—i.e. "away from home"—give you the emotional space to write?

I live in the Midwest, in a college town that is at the heart of the literary world in America. Everyone I know is writing a book, a story, an essay, a poem, an article. It's rather amazing and frightening: all that talent in snow-bound Iowa. I always say it's a good place to work because whatever can you do with five months of winter except stay indoors and think? Having said that, most of my work is 'set' in Alabama, in the small towns and rural areas that I now visit. I miss the kind of dailiness of actually living in the place I write about. You don't quite get the same thing in a two-week visit in the summer. As a result, I'm setting a new novel in Iowa AND Alabama, because I want to use both environments (and the temperament of their people) to best advantage.

I'm currently making myself crazy by working on several books. I got an award from the University of Iowa to do research on a book titled *Smart Girls*. In this book I'm examining the lives of intellectually gifted girls (between the ages of 17-29) who have wrestled with the psychological claims of ambition, creativity and intellectual risk. In my own life, the right to 'claim' ambition was a difficult step and I want to understand the benefits and risks of ambition for young girls today.

I'm also working on a book of short stories, much to my surprise! I spent much of the summer writing essays, then suddenly felt the tug of stories. I love stories and when they come, I just go with them. Many characters: an old grandfather, a young anorexic girl, a cheerleader, an older woman whose husband is dying, a young doctor in World War II.

Much to my horror, I'm also re-writing a novel. I say horror because I so wanted to be finished with it last year. It had to wait—and necessarily so—while I finished a few other pieces.

Do you have a list of writers who are under-rated?

I don't know if I would call these writers under-rated, but there are several books   I've read this past year I'd love to pass on. Two memoirs I read recently are *Before the Knife*, Carolyn Slaughter, and *An American Requiem*, James Carroll (both in paperback). I just heard the poet Bruce Beasley read from *Signs and Abominations*, and he was sensational. I'd also recommend two books of fiction: *You Are Not a Stranger Here*, Adam Haslett, and *Still She Haunts Me*, Katie Roiphe (a novel about Lewis Carroll and Alice Liddell). All lovely books!

Selected bibliography of Patricia Foster

Non-fiction:

Minding the Body (editor)
Sister to Sister (editor)
The Healing Circle (co-editor along with Mary Swander)
All The Lost Girls: Confessions of a Southern Daughter
Just Beneath My Skin: Autobiography and Self-Discovery

William Price Fox

William Price Fox dislikes being compared to anyone else or pigeon-holed. He tries to make every book different from the one before. In the last thirty-plus years he's written for *Sports Illustrated, Golf Digest, Harper's,* and *Esquire.* His fiction includes *Wild Blue Yonder, Dixiana Moon, Southern Fried,* and *Ruby Red.* Fox teaches creative writing at the University of South Carolina in his native Columbia. He is married to humorist Sarah Gilbert.

Wild Blue Yonder is being promoted as an "autobiographical" book. How much of the novel is truth?

Most of it is true. I've changed a lot. I did go into the service at seventeen. I did quit high school. I was in trouble. I wanted to fly and I did not want to be sent home. I was a Lieutenant. I have three brothers—I took them out of the book. The ending was certainly based on the truth.

Your father looms large in your work, particularly _Wild Blue Yonder_ and _Dixiana Moon._ Was he larger than life?

Fathers loom large for men. My father did go to jail. He was a moon-shiner and a musician. While my dad was in the navy, he met my mom. She was a nightclub hostess in Chicago. They worked in restaurants down South. My dad played the trumpet, the guitar, and the piano. He sang. He was a member of a half-white, half-black band. They called themselves "The Hawaiians" and sang in Spanish.

Talk about your experience as a cadet during World War II.

The cadets were very hard, very strict. I decided to be relaxed. I volunteered for what no one else would do because I did not want to wash out or be sent home. I watched and saw men try too hard and screw up. I took that as a lesson. We lost a lot of people in training. There were hatch marks on the door reading, "cut here to open." We thought it was funny. We lost almost all of our squad. Bill Clinton was right when he said, "When these people were kids, they saved the world."

When did you come to writing?

I started writing in my thirties. I was in sales in New York for eight years. I liked my income and was afraid to quit. I used to drink in the White Horse Tavern. I met Delmore Schwartz, Dylan Thomas, Norman Mailer...I was part of the "Saloon Society" in the Village. One night one of my friends was too drunk to write his column for *The Village Voice*. I wrote a column describing a Southerner who came to New York, stayed in the Heart of Dixie Hotel, spent all of his time on one block, and who went home repeating the cliché "I wouldn't want to live there." I was suspicious about writing because it was easy to write.

You've spent some time in Hollywood...

I went to Hollywood to write for "The Beverly Hillbillies" which embarrasses me now. Paul Henning had the rights to everything all tied up. He also controlled "Petticoat Junction." People were very greedy about credits.

I worked, with Walter Tevis, on the screenplay of *The Man Who Fell To Earth*. I took my name off of the script when the check bounced.

I worked with Norman Lear on the script for *Cold Turkey*.

I am still a member of the Writer's Guild.

I like Hollywood but I couldn't write fiction there because it took too much time to collaborate on writing.

I left Hollywood to go back to New York eventually replacing Kurt Vonnegut at Iowa. I knew Walter Tevis from Iowa and spent six years (1967-1973) there.

You have a kind of cult following in the South.

(Laughing) That's better than NO following. Everything I do is different. I also have a big following in golf writing. I write for myself.

What would you still like to do?

(Laughter) I'm doing it.

I want to write funny. I don't want to underline what I'm doing. I dislike pushing humor. I want the undercut to be sharp.

I'm working on a novel tentatively titled *Smoke* which is based on my experience in sales.

I spent time with Satchel Paige and am working on a stage show about the experience.

I teach two days a week. I do only what I want to do. Financially, I squeak by.

What's teaching like for you?

If a student has no sense of humor, I'm suspicious. They all use computers now. It ruins their prose style because they stop and correct. They lose their rhythm and flow. I tell them to type for ten minutes with a blackened screen with no sound. Then try to write once they get a good sound going.

What advice do you offer novice writers?

Forget punctuation and spelling.
Look for the phrasing.
Read Jane Austen and Flannery O'Connor.
Establish character in a hurry.
Show rather than tell.
Undercut comedy.

Selected bibliography of William Price Fox

Fiction:

Moonshine Light, Moonshine Bright
Ruby Red
Dixianna Moon
Wild Blue Yonder
Satchel Paige's America
Southern Fried Plus Six
Doctor Golf
Golfing in the Carolinas
Lunatic Wind (formerly known as *Hurricane Hugo: Storm of the Century)*
How 'Bout Them Gamecocks'

H.E. Francis

H. E. ("Herb") Francis has an enviable existence—he's spent most of his professional life teaching, writing, translating, and traveling. He's received three Fulbright fellowships to Argentina where he's met some of the most outstanding writers of a generation. The author of ten previous books, Francis's most recent collection of short stories, *I'll Never Leave You*, was selected for the G.S. Sharat Chandra Prize for Short Fiction by Diane Glancy. His earlier work, which includes *Goya, Are You With Me Now?* and *The Invisible Country*, has been praised by Joyce Carol Oates, Harry Crews, John Hawkes, Malcolm Cowley, Anne Tyler, and Kelly Cherry. His stories have been included in the *Pushcart, O. Henry*, and *Best American Short Stories* volumes. His book *The Itinerary of Beggars* won the Iowa School of Letters Award for Short Fiction, and his book *Naming Things* was selected for the Illinois Short Fiction Series. Professor Emeritus at the University of Alabama at Huntsville, Francis divides his time between Madrid, Spain, and Huntsville.

Would you like to talk about your personal life?

I've lived for fifty-five years in the South, but till I enlisted in the Army Air Force in World War II, my early roots thrived in a New England town under the influence of what to me was a Hawthorne–Melville world happily combined with the spontaneous temperament of a population of Italian and Portuguese cotton and mill workers. Before enlisting I worked in a zipper factory, in accounting. Being thrown in with other G.I.s educated me, knocked my pride, made me feel like anybody, and ignited my natural passion. After the war, on the G.I. Bill, I went to the University of Wisconsin, then home to Brown, then to begin…

How did you come to teach at the University of Alabama at Huntsville? How long were you there?

I fell into the academic life, the last thing I ever thought I'd do; but I discovered that part of me was born for it—Penn State, Illinois, University of Tennessee at Knoxville, Emory, and UAH (23 years). One day in my first lit class I saw what I would call the "skeleton" under the story. The next morning I sat down in my rented room in Harrisburg from eight till eight and wrote my first story and sent it off. *Prairie Schooner* accepted it, and I've been at it ever since, wherever I am, from seven until eleven every morning of my life. UAH, when I was hired from Argentina, was generous, promised classes afternoons and nights, with mornings free, and kept the promise, always. The university was tiny, "being born." I worked with great teachers determined to make it a great department. They succeeded.

In what ways has living in the South influenced your writing?

The South is one of my places. Does that sound strange? It shouldn't. Place makes. Place grips and roots you down. You can have more than one place over a lifetime; and depending on your sensibility and experience, your capacity for absorbing and empathizing, you absorb place. New England and Long Island formed my early life, but long experience in the South, England, Argentina, and Spain keep transforming my "self." The South (as the war did) gave me objectivity about my past, place, history; also its diction sharpened my ear, heightened my feeling for my mythic town, sharpened my sense of isolation, attracted me to the communal, though its remarkable humor I found inimitable.

Has Southern literature changed in the years you've lived here?

Yes. Unlike that of Caldwell, Faulkner, Welty, it has become self-consciously "Southern," a designation nurtured by editors and publishers, a commerce that plays falsely on the regional.

You split your time between Huntsville and Madrid. Would you like to discuss the pleasures of living in two places, two countries?

In Spain time is visible in what man has created over the centuries (time in America is visible in nature). The past is a living presence—lived in, adapted for use, alive now. After years of reading Spanish literature and teaching and living in Spanish countries, I feel a deep kinship with the Spanish nature, more overtly emotional and expressive, the Spaniard's fervent defense of the self, his youth; and I revel in the rich cross-countries' culture which has invaded Spain since Franco died. In the European Union, despite its problems, I feel I am living in the ambience of a tolerant new world, and that I have come from an old one. Think of the Union, based on our democratic model of states, but as a more ambitious democracy of nations.

Is it possible for regional literature to reflect a broader worldview? Could you offer a working definition of what constitutes "regional?"

"Regional" vanishes when a writer so penetrates human nature that its truths apply to people anywhere. Set against World War II, Welty's "Why I Live at the P.O." dramatizes how war comes between two people, two nations, and among many nations. A writer may never leave town, yet become international through his perceptions of human nature. There are some exceptional writers of an authentic South writing now; there are those whose folksy stories, set in backwater towns and villages, follow in the wake of Faulkner and others. The best writers, like Bobbie Ann Mason, write American stories set in the South.

Do you think of yourself primarily as a short story writer or novelist?

Oh, there are early, trial novels in the bottom drawer, where they'll stay! Usually I tend to see large things in small incidents. Writing a short story is like tearing a scene complete in itself from a large tapestry, its threads suggesting its further reaches. But the needs of a situation determine a work's length.

Talk about your work as a translator.

Though I've translated a couple of hundred stories, three books, some poetry, by some of the best of writers, I'm not a professional translator. I am free to translate what I love. Translating keeps Spanish, Spain, and my friends alive in me. I get "inside" the writer and his world, and it expands my understanding of his world and my own. Spanish rhythms and syntax have crept into my style, and my deep feeling for Spanish has impelled me to create fictional characters set in that world. My most treasured comment came from a critic who said my Argentine stories seemed written by a native.

I translate only a few writers—because they are the finest Argentine writers of their generation: Antonia Di Benedetto, Daniel Moyano, Juan Jose Hernandez, and the younger Norberto Luis Romero. I don't translate a writer because he is a friend, but because I believe in the nature and quality of his work.

Do you see any similarities between Latin American, Spanish, and Southern writers?

Faulkner is the single greatest outside influence on writers of the Hispanic "boom" with his burgeoning language, his concentration on the *loca*, his creation of a mythic, literary place, a certain measure of the grotesque, and fantastic (Gothic in form, here; magic realism, there) combined with the historically credible—an influence openly admitted by Garcia-Marquez, Juan Benet, Juan Carlos Onetti, and others. One night Onetti asked me what Faulkner's greatest story was. I said, "To me, 'Barn Burning.' " He said at once, "All the Dead Pilots," a shock to me, and added, "And my translation of that story is the best in the Spanish language." I was steeped in Onetti's work. Back in Huntsville, I translated his story, "Esbjerg, on the Coast" and after ninety days of going over it, I sent it to him with a note that I was returning the favor he'd done Faulkner. My reward when I saw him in Madrid: "This is the best English translation of any of my works."

Who are/were your mentors?

My greatest mentor was my grandfather. He exemplified raw life—incredible tragedy and suffering, maimed in body, strengthened in character and spirit, a sometime itinerant preacher. He early stirred in me a kind of Dostoyevskian awareness of human suffering. At Wisconsin, the owner of a pharmacy, who dreamed of being a professor, at forty, sent his daughter off to the Sorbonne, sold his business, worked on a PhD in English. That impassioned Henry Mann (my grandfather) taught me Milton, hummed Beethoven to Milton, hence my undying passion for Milton's language. Two great Spanish professors—Antonio Sanchez-Barbudo and the novelist Arturo Barea, both exiles under Franco—fostered my love of Spanish literature. Strangely, most of the great things in my life have come through my association with the Spanish—my student Fulbright to Oxford, three Fulbright grants to Argentina, my adoption of an Argentine boy (with now eight grandchildren and several greats), the publication of my first collection of stories set in Spanish, meeting Argentine writers whom I would translate, my move to Spain with my friends exiled under the Argentine dictator Videla, and my actual life in Spain. As I tell my friends, with this dual life, I envy myself!

What books or writers influenced you?

Hard to say. I taught world literature. Literature builds on literature. I'm an insane re-reader: James forever, Conrad, Lawrence, Woolf, Thomas Bernard, Patrick White, Cela, Proust, and much modern European and Oriental literature as well as hosts of poets. Pessoa, Salinas, Yeats, Hopkins, Vallejo...I sometimes find, when reading my work over, I have echoed phrases or lines from their works. I leave them. They are my heritage.

Where do you see your work fitting into contemporary literature?

I wouldn't attempt to say. I have written through decades, not been labeled or pinned down. I may be part of the increasing incorporation of the international—language and subject—into the American world of letters. I am merely one more in the human tide.

How would you define what it means to live one's life as a writer? An artist?

It means to have, through imagination, a way for the mind to wrestle with the totality of things and rescue from it some human dignity. As an artist? Never to flinch at what is human. Never to cease seeking the best forms to contain its essence.

Did you have a theme in mind before your wrote the stories in *I'll Never Leave You*?

I don't think that way. I'm very intuitive and have a certain empathy with characters, which evokes the actions, and I follow them, trying to depict their inner lives, that "invisible country" which tempts me into them. There is so much in the well of us and I try to follow it into that sometimes forbidden territory which many of us do not want to venture into, where sometimes deep sufferings may lead us ultimately to the most rewarding moments of our lives, to revelations of the self or shifting and evasive selves or the unself in us. I am concerned at the time of writing with the underlying motion of the experience; a real experience will always suggest where the motion leads us, to what ambiguities—not obscurities, but meaningful ambiguities.

In "Boulders" you chose to eliminate quotation marks and most dialogue attributions...

Many writers eliminate and vary punctuation—this is common. Each story demands its own total form. I feel that, in a strange way, a story "demands," dictates, its experience. I don't think it out ahead. I am so involved with the characters that I have to wait for the first line, usually have to hear the rhythm, and when I do, I can go on. Otherwise, I am stymied. I have to go on then and let the story fulfill itself, which means the experience undertaken determines what it will become—story, novella, novel.

Diane Glancy, who selected your book for the Chandra Prize, wrote that she liked "the solid stories"... and the more experimental "turned loose" writing that marbles the collection. How do you feel your work has evolved over the years?

My language has always been naturally somewhat poetic—I have had to work very hard to curb that impulse when it was misleading, misapplied, not appropriate. There has always been a certain "peripheral" effect in my work...I have maintained that, but I hope I have turned it into a rich suggestiveness. I have also absorbed foreign idioms and their rhythms into my own English rhythms though that may be really evident, and justly so, more to the writer. Of course, my ventures make sometimes extreme, sometimes absurd (risky), situations turn into an emotive reality, accepted through knowing.

**What would you like for readers, and writers, to garner from
*I'll Never Leave You?***

I hope any good or great literature will, even if it is only
during the reading, remind a reader of his own humanity. For a
writer? There is always the evocation of someone immersed in
common challenges to render the fictional life with all his
honesty. That achievement is enough to give fever and inspire.

Selected bibliography of H.E. Francis

Fiction:

The Invisible Country
Goya, Are You With Me Now?
The Sudden Trees
A Disturbance of Gulls
Had
The History of A Man In Despair
The Itinerary of Beggars
Naming Things

Vanessa Davis Griggs

In many ways, Vanessa Davis Griggs' life is much like that of her characters. She understands what it means to have a good work ethic, to get knocked down and get back up, and to trust her instincts. Her innate spirituality and passionate nature form both her personal and writing life.

What have you been doing since the publication of *Promises Beyond Jordan*?

Oh wow, a lot has transpired since our last interview. Black Entertainment Television Books/New Spirit (their inspirational imprint) acquired the rights to my originally self-published novel, *Promises Beyond Jordan*. I signed a two-book deal with them and they re-released *Promises Beyond Jordan* with a new cover February 2004. My second release, *Wings of Grace*, hit the stands February 2005. I'm still writing, speaking, and enjoying what I do with great passion.

Tell readers about the connection between *Promises Beyond Jordan* and *Wings of Grace*. Do you anticipate writing a third novel in the series?

Wings of Grace begins where *Promises Beyond Jordan* left off. Because I'm not fond of reruns, any follow-up of a book I do has to be fresh with some new faces and new things happening just to keep me engaged and excited as I pen it. You will recognize some characters from *Promises Beyond Jordan* in *Wings of Grace*, but many of the new players are "characters" indeed! I have learned from early feedback of *Wings of Grace* that you can actually read it without having read *Promises Beyond Jordan*. But if you read (or have read) *Promises Beyond Jordan* first, you're going to be in for a treat, witnessing a few characters' evolutions. I do anticipate a third and even fourth novel in what has now taken off to become an inspiring series.

Has the act of writing become any easier with practice? With publication? With acclaim?

Practice does make one better, no matter the task at hand. I'm a strange type of writer when it comes to my personal writing process. I don't write every day in the sense of sitting down at the keyboard, but my method of formulating situations and scenarios in my head, observing, and jotting down thoughts and scenes when they flood my soul, all are part of writing for me. Publication can add some pressure when you're writing the next book if more people have a hand and a stake in it. In my case, I don't care to write a book just to write one. If I can't create a story that I believe will be my best work to date, I'm not going to just cookie-cut a story to make money or meet someone else's assigned deadline. The passion in and for the book begins with me. If I'm not feeling it, I don't do it. With acclaim? I'm still Vanessa who has big dreams, and I am honored when people read my work. People don't have to pick it up or read it, you know. My desire is always to give my best in whatsoever things I do.

How did you get "hooked-up" with BET? Talk about the experience. Your reaction.

I published *Promises Beyond Jordan* under my own press. It was selling okay when the senior editor at BET Books read it and called my publishing company's number in January 2003 to get my personal number so she could get in touch with me. When she discovered I was one and the same, she told me how much she enjoyed *Promises Beyond Jordan* and she wanted to talk with me about possibly acquiring it. She offered me a two-book deal, which made way for *Wings of Grace* to hit the scene through them.

Do you see yourself as writing for any one particular market?

Since I've acquired a reputation for writing in multiple genres simultaneously, I don't see my style changing. It's just part of my DNA. I like to write the way we as people live life. There are multiple aspects to our lives; I think in order for fiction to ring true, it should mirror real life. There will always be some aspects of Christian, mystery/suspense, possibly sprigs of history, romance, and multicultural in my work. All of this works for me. It keeps me from being bored.

What's been the most pleasant/least pleasant experience in promoting your work?

Most pleasant has got to be meeting some great people whether it's in person, through email, snail mail, or chatting on the phone. I do lots of interviews and I've met some people who remain in my life, even to this day. Least pleasant would be the people I meet who feel it's their God-ordained calling to tear me down or put me in my place. I don't run into those kinds often, but they are lurking out there. It's also a bit frustrating sometimes trying to get into a few places if you're not a big name, but that just causes me to press harder or figure out other ways to do what needs to be done. Perseverance, that's all it develops in me.

How difficult is it to convincingly write about faith?

It's not difficult for me to write about faith because it's part of my make-up. You have to be careful when using the word faith though, because I think all people have faith. There are some who have faith that they can do, and they do. There are some who have faith that they can't do, and they don't. Both are faith; both are working. People must be alert when using faith. Now faith in God is what I love, and that's easy for me to write about because I know how we are as people. We all face challenges at one time or another and things may not always work out the way we would like. Then there are other times when we know that we know that we know! Now that's a faith to "write home" about.

Did you start *Wings of Grace* with an image, a character, or a plot device in mind? Which comes first for you?

I generally begin a book with a question that gnaws at me. I find myself churning it around in my head. It's like asking a question that's out there and waiting for the answer to reveal itself to me. Then images come and my characters appear, letting me know who they are and what (in their opinion) is going on. I hear them speak in their own voices, telling their part of the tale. It's quite fascinating for me. The plot usually is a skeleton with the meat being added on as the story begins to move forward (*Wings of Grace* is a bit big-boned). That's why I actually hate writing out a full outline (some publishers want it) where I have to tell everything that happens. There are some things I don't know and don't want to know until it bleeds out on the paper. I get my joy out of writing it and finding out things that even I, as the author, didn't know. That's why I'll let the publisher know if they want an outline that things are subject (and most likely) to change.

Who are your influences?

My influences are those who live life with passion and with a spirit of excellence. I like people who are honest with life. My influences are those who have vision and go after their dreams, demonstrating that it's indeed possible. I believe if they can do it, then so can I. My influences have been my mother and my father; some of the elderly with their fascinating quirks, fantastic mannerisms, and wisdom; and children with their pureness of innocence. People you might never have heard of before, but great people who've had a finger in who I am now. From a literary standpoint, it would probably be Ernest J. Gaines, Toni Morrison, Og Mandino, and Barbara Taylor Bradford (with *A Woman of Substance*) because I see their efforts in the telling of the tale. I learned early in life to encourage and influence myself.

That's important: Learn to encourage, influence, and believe in yourself.

What would you still like to be asked about your work? Yourself?

What motivates you? That would be the question. What makes me keep going when I have so many reasons (justifiably so) to quit? What motivates me is my knowing that others believe in me; that they are cheering me on. My relationship with God who lets me know He is faithful. I love when I know He has told me something, and I watch Him do what—to the world—seems most likely impossible. I figure if God believed in me so much that He chose me, the least I can do is listen to what He says and follow His every lead. My other motivation is knowing others are watching me, and I want them to see me continuing on in genuine faith. I want someone who desires to embark on a thing (or if they already have), and they feel like quitting because it's tough, to look at me and say: If she did it, so can I. I want to make a positive difference in someone else's life, other than just my own. Trust me: When I do what I do, it's not always about me.

Selected bibliography of Vanessa Davis Griggs

Fiction:

Destiny Unlimited
The Rose of Jericho
Promises Beyond Jordan
Wings of Grace

Tim Gautreaux

Tim Gautreaux's first novel, *The Next Step in the Dance*, won the 1999 Southeastern Booksellers Award. Born and reared in Louisiana, the author recently retired from his position as Writer-in-Residence at Southeastern Louisiana University and has spent the last few months researching his next novel. His work has been selected for inclusion in the *O. Henry* and *Best American Short Story Annuals* and has appeared in *Zoetrope, GQ, Harper's,* and *The Atlantic Monthly.*

You're from Louisiana...

I was born in 1947 in Morgan City, a tough oil-patch town in South-Central Louisiana. My father was a tugboat captain, and he wanted me to follow in his footsteps, but the job was too slow for me. After twelve years in a Catholic school and four years in a regional college, I entered an accelerated PhD program at the University of South Carolina where I studied under James Dickey for three years. PhD in hand, I got a job teaching literature and creative writing at Southeastern Louisiana University, taught thirty years and retired last December.

What changes have you seen in the state and local culture during your lifetime?

In South Louisiana, when I was a child, more people spoke French, but the number of French-speakers has declined a great deal in the past thirty years. Cajuns were shy about their culture, suspecting that it was kind of a joke to outlanders, and many didn't pass on the language. I didn't even realize I was a Cajun until I moved out of state to go to graduate school. Nobody talked about being this or that in those days. Nowadays Cajuns are pretty knowledgeable about their history, and though the language has diminished, the music, food, and folkways are thriving here in Louisiana and around the country. Louisiana has developed more of a literary presence also thanks to writers like John Biguenet, James Lee Burke, Walker Percy, Andre Dubus, Shirley Ann Grau and a dozen others.

What image or character came to mind first as you were writing *The Clearing*?

The constable. I imagined his haunted expression as he looked out across the sawmill yard toward the saloon, hearing the yowls of a brawl and knowing that the only way he could save the fighters from themselves was to hurt at least one of them, even though he didn't want to.

Did you do any research for the historical elements or were they part of local and/or family lore?

The meaningful details in *The Clearing* came out of my imagination, supported by thousands of bits and pieces of things I heard as a child: a reference to a long-dead relative, an old firearm in the closet purported to have killed someone, an embarrassed turn of the head, a helpless shrug, the way an uncle slowed down his voice when speaking two sentences about what he did in the war.

One thing that makes a child turn into a writer is the ability to understand the importance of remembering everything. And to remember you have to listen and believe that everything you hear is interesting.

When I was a kid, a lot of old relatives were still around and they talked and talked about their jobs, local murders, cops, cancer, lynchings, saw milling, how to repair steam engines, being poisoned by a pork roast, killing pigeons, praying, water-skiing, steamboat navigation, and welding.

I consulted my library of antique machinery manuals and catalogs, read a book or two on saw milling history, but the guts of the story came from shutting up and listening.

Would you talk about "Writing about the bonds between men without succumbing to sentimentality?"

Avoiding sentimentality is easy to do. Use not one cliché. Use as little exposition as possible. Focus on action and detail that in a subtle way suggests what you want to say.

Were you influenced by any particular writers?

Flannery O'Connor (who hasn't been?), Walker Percy, Jane Austen, Cormac McCarthy, Annie Proulx.

Would you like to name some writers that readers should be reading but might have missed?

William Gay, Tom Franklin, George Saunders, Jeffrey Lent, and Kent Haruf.

Does teaching influence your writing in any way?

Sure. When I teach a room full of students, I teach myself, remind myself. One time a negative review charged that I must listen to my own lectures. I would hope so.

You've spent the summer promoting the book. What was your impression of the state of bookselling? Reading?

The independent booksellers are the saviours and maintainers of literary fiction. They actually read the books, make recommendations, do each customer a favor by matching that customer's individual taste up with a particular writer, plus they sometimes challenge their customer's laziness and recommend titles that engage the intellect. Again, they read the books and recommend from experience. A chain store clerk can only ask "You want fries with that?"

What would you still like to be asked?

"Why is there so damn much machinery in everything you write?"

I'm sure someone will write a master's thesis on that topic, and I don't really understand why myself, fully. I've always been fascinated by any mechanism and love to take lawnmowers and tractors and steam locomotives apart to make them run better.

When I started working on the accordion scene in *The Clearing*, I bought a big accordion for fifty bucks on Ebay, taught myself to play "Lady of Spain" with one finger, figured out the stops and buttons, discovered how the thing smelled, vibrated on my chest, broke my back, wrenched my shoulders, confused my fingers with its left-hand board of 120 identical black chord buttons. Then I took it out to my machine shop and completely dismantled it and figured out how it worked, studied the brass reeds, beeswax, kid-leather check valves, etc.

The thing about a properly designed mechanism is that there are no non-functioning parts. Everything has a purpose, every bit and tag, screw and eyelet. Good fiction's the same way.

Selected bibliography of Tim Gautreaux

Fiction:

The Clearing
The Next Step in the Dance
Same Place, Same Things
Welding With Children: Stories

Carolyn Haines

If Carolyn Haines had not wanted to be a writer, she could have had a career in stand-up comedy. Her sense of humor and timing are impeccable. She's written romantic suspense as well as mysteries. Her "Bones" mysteries are anticipated by readers and have delighted reviewers. Eugene Walter, a mentor and dear friend, encouraged Haines' early efforts. We should all have such "literary" guardian angels.

You had an unusual wedding.

On January 11, 2003, in my front yard, riding my magnificent steed Cogar, I married Steve Greene, a captain in the Jefferson County Sheriff's Department (talk about life imitating art!). I met Steve doing research for a book. He went to college on writing scholarships and then went into law enforcement. I needed some help with some forensics for my mystery series. Steve rode his horse, Rio. Instead of a wedding party, we had horse wranglers. And about ten people gave me away.

You've worked in several genres—romance, mystery, and journalism. Would you like to compare the experiences? Readership? How each type of book is promoted?

My parents were journalists, and I grew up with "ink in the blood." I truly loved journalism, but the truth is, my mother was the true reporter in the family. My dad was an editor. I was a feature writer who was also a photographer. I did some investigative stuff and some political writing, but I loved bending the language to create rhythms and images. I liked telling the stories of people's lives. Folks call it soft news (in contrast to the more prestigious hard news) but it was the writing I realized I loved, more than the reporting. I always wanted to write fiction, but my dad told me that I needed a career. Journalism was a career. Fiction writing was a gamble. So I begin writing fiction while I had a full-time job as a journalist. I wrote only for myself, and I wrote short fiction. I was besotted with Flannery O'Connor, Eudora Welty, Jayne Anne Philips.

I just didn't realize that publishing a short story is harder than finding hen's teeth on a rooster. So, I began looking at what people read, and romance was the best selling market. I read some, underestimated the skill required, and set to writing. I quickly learned that I didn't have the skill for focusing the story strictly on romance. Thank goodness Harlequin started publishing their Intrigue line, which features romance and mystery. I finally had a format where I could blend what I liked— good characterization with plot.

As I grow as a writer, I'm more and more fascinated with plot and structure. These are the hardest elements for me, therefore the most challenging. In my own mind, my career is a natural progression. In all of the areas I've written, I've been able to use language to create a unique place and unique people. Today, Sarah Booth and the people of Zinnia are as real to me as my relatives. (And far better behaved, I might point out.)

What changes have you seen in the attitudes toward women writers, editors, and publishers during your career?

Working with the publishers I've worked with— Harlequin, Pinnacle, Dutton and Bantam—I have to say that I've worked almost exclusively with women...I have been overwhelmed by the professionalism of the women. I probably shouldn't admit this because it is such a foolish prejudice, but when I went to my first Romance Writers Conference, I went as a journalist. And I realized that this wasn't some fuzzy slippers and bathrobe crowd. These ladies were pros. And they were generous pros who took time to talk to wannabes. There are jerks everywhere, but for the most part, the women I've met in the business are smart, upfront, and fun gals. So how has that changed since 1988 when I first published? I think that women are taken more seriously now because they are such a big part of the market. And they've made certain that bookstores and booksellers know that.

In certain circles it is still a tightly held belief that women don't have anything interesting to say, but I don't think that kind of prejudice will ever go away. Ignorance will forever be with us.

Talk about moving between genres and mention the names under which you write.

At Harlequin Intrigue I write under Caroline Burnes. At Pinnacle (one book, *A Woman in Jeopardy*), at Dutton and now at Bantam, I use my legal name, Carolyn Haines. And I did a book about my brother. It's fictional, but wicked. So just for fun I took the name Lizzie Hart. It was all tongue-in-cheek. I'm finishing a horror screenplay now (my first). Should it turn out to be any good, I'll probably use initials to avoid the impression of a female writer. Why, you ask? Because I think it's an easier sell in horror if the writer is perceived as a guy. I don't have statistics on this, but it's just a gut feeling.

I grew up reading off a carousel rack in the drugstore where I worked after school. The jobber stocked the racks every month, and I could read anything I wanted as long as I didn't break the spine or damage the book. I read Thomas Williams along with Harold Robbins. There wasn't anyone to tell me that this was great literature and this was trash. I just read everything. I'm still like that today. I read a lot of different genres, and the only thing I demand is that the writing is good. I don't read poorly written stuff no matter what the genre or who the writer is.

Talk about starting your own publishing company.

I had a dream...seriously. I saw so many of my friends in mid-list getting squelched and squeezed. They were fine writers, but no one had ever heard of them. So I thought, maybe a little book company could focus on one book and really make it happen. You know, just put everything into one book and push really hard. My idea was that an independent book publisher might be able to hook up with the independent bookstores and make a real difference. To test the water, I did one of my own books (*Shop Talk*, by Lizzie Hart). No one warned me that satire was hard to market. And, of course, I had no idea how to run a business and I had no desire to learn about licenses and taxes and all of that icky stuff that is part of small businesshood. But I was determined. I wanted to try it, because I thought it was something important to do. And I hooked up with some really smart women in an organization called The Authors Studio who gave me the benefit of their knowledge. I published *Shop Talk*, and then realized that I had no way to get it into bookstores. The chains would only order through a couple of big distributors, who wanted about a 55 percent discount. I had to pay shipping. They could return books and I had to pay shipping back. The independent bookstores I'd hoped would read my book and hand-sell it were fighting for their lives. It was as much trouble to order one title from me as it was to order a hundred from a distributor. I wasn't in a position where I could make myself a big winner, and I realized it after about 10 months.

I have to say my agent sold the right to *Shop Talk* to a Japanese publisher (I still grin when I think about them reading about these crazy Mississippians). And I published a second, non-fiction book called *Moments with Eugene...A Collection of Memories*. Rebecca Barrett and I edited some 60 submissions about Mobile writer Eugene Walter. He was a magnificent writer, a wonderful man, and a dear friend. He was also crazy as a run-over dog—in the finest Southern sense, of course. He worked on Fellini films and lived life by his own terms. Yet he was so generous to other writers. So we did that book and then closed the press. I hated the business end of it. I didn't like writing invoices or keeping up with things, but you just have to do it or the taxman will take you to prison. I'm just not a businessperson.

I don't regret any of it. I worked very hard, because I had a full-time job and I was also writing books for New York publishers. But would I do it again? No. Not knowing how difficult it is. But it did give me a new respect for what publishers have to do to get the smallest attention for a book. Just doing press releases for *Shop Talk* taught me a lot. In that regard, I'm a better professional, I think.

What problems do women face in publishing? Have you dealt with problems you're convinced a man would never have to face?

My agent, Marian Young, and I talk about this. I sometimes get a little chip on my shoulder, but she says it's tough for everyone, not just women. I think mostly it has to do with "a prophet in his own town" thing.

In the last two years, I've met some terrific writers. These are guy writers, and they let me into the club. Last October, Les Standiford invited me to teach at Seaside, a conference that's held every year in Seaside, Florida and sponsored by Florida International University. Dennis Lehane, one of Les's students, was also a presenter. It was the most refreshing thing to find myself, writer-to-writer, talking with these authors whose work I absolutely respected. This was fun. This is how it should be. But I have to say that at the same meeting were Lynne Barrett and Patricia Foster, women writers I greatly admire. We weren't these creatures of gender—we were writers teaching and talking about writing. It was one of the best experiences I've ever had. Maybe I'm just getting older, or maybe I'm keeping better company, but I like the place I'm moving to.

Let's talk about your background. Where did you grow up? Where do you live now? Where were you educated?

I was raised in Lucedale, Mississippi, about 40 miles from where I currently live in Semmes, Alabama. (Just across the Escatawpa River). Lucedale was a town of about 3,000 when I lived there. I think my generation of small-town Southerners may have had the last golden childhood. We rode our bikes through town at 2 a.m., without a single fear of a predator or some deviant. I picked peas as a five-year-old with the town police chief (and only officer at the time). And I learned to swim in an amber river with my brothers and my dog. All of this is very much a part of my writing. I wanted a horse so bad I actually prayed my mother would give birth to one (instead it was a brother). I wanted to be a cowgirl, and I was a tomboy. And I still live that life. I have six horses, four dogs, five cats and a small farm. I love to just get out in the woods and think—on horseback or foot.

I went to high school at George County High (which, much to my chagrin, has just banned *Of Mice and Men*. I know, it just makes me sick) and I went to the University of Southern Mississippi for a BS in journalism. Later I went to the University of South Alabama for an MA in English with emphasis in creative writing.

Humor is one of your trademarks...

I guess if you don't learn to laugh at life a little, it's going to be a long hard trek. I like humor, and I enjoy writing it, especially if it's just a little barbed. My family history is filled with these tragic stories that are hilarious. They're so awful, but they are just too funny. So we tell them around family gatherings and groan and laugh and weep because that's just life as we know it.

Did you have mentors when you were getting started in the writing business? Do you think men or women make better mentors?

I had two teachers at USM, Gordon Weaver and Jean Todd Freeman, who encouraged me to write fiction. I was on a journalism track, but I took a few classes in fiction writing as electives. They did tell me I had talent. They urged me to write. Through the years, I've kept in touch with both of them on a sporadic basis. It is true that one good teacher can change the fate of a student. In those early days of rejection, the praise that Dr. Weaver and Ms. Freeman gave me sustained me. And I have to say that Tahti Carter, an editor at Intrigue, saved me from quitting. I owe a lot to Tahti. She is a brilliant editor, and she pulled me out of the slagheap and bought my first book. And, of course, Eugene Walter encouraged me in the early '80s when I met him. We'd drink champagne and toast marshmallows over candles and he'd tell me about working for the *Paris Review* and living in Rome and how the only important thing was to write. He said that he saw greatness in me. Do you know what kind of impact those words can have on a young writer with no hope? Let's just say that money can't buy such emotional power.

As to gender, it's hard to say. I don't think it's a gender issue. I do think it's a matter of generosity of spirit. There are generous writers, and there are those who spew only acid and cruelty. Stay away from the latter.

What question have you always wanted to be asked in an interview?

"What were you in a past life?"

I was an American Indian who could ride any horse in the Dakotas bareback. And I understood my relationship with this planet in a way I'm still trying to retrieve in this lifetime.

Selected bibliography Carolyn Haines

Fiction:

Them Bones
Touched
Crossed Bones
Splintered Bones
Buried Bones
Judas Burning
Hallowed Bones
Summer of the Redeemers
Shop Talk
Penumbra
Bone to Pick
Summer of Fear

Non-fiction:

My Mother's Witness: The Peggy Morgan Story
Moments with Eugene…A Collection of Memories (co-edited with Rebecca Barnett)

Joy Harjo

Joy Harjo belongs to the Muscogee Nation and is the author of seven collections of poetry, most recently *How We Became Human: New and Selected Poems: 1975-2001*. She was named winner of the Arrell Gibson Lifetime Achievement Award from the Oklahoma Center for the Book in 2003. The award recognizes a body of work contributing to Oklahoma's literary heritage.

Where did you grow up? At what age did you know that you wanted to be a writer/artist/musician?

I grew up in Tulsa, Oklahoma. I knew from the beginning that I wanted to be an artist. My first urges were to draw and sing. My grandmother Naomi Harjo was a painter and we had her paintings in our house. I found great refuge in the act of drawing—to move into that creative space engaged my spirit in a way nothing else did at that very young age. I got in trouble for decorating the walls of the garage with chalk drawings. I also covered the closet of the kid's bedroom with my art. My mother was the singer, so we had music and her voice often holding our home together. I loved listening, and loved singing—privately. When other girl children my age were making plans to be teachers, nurses and brides (yes brides)—I was always the only one who wanted to be an artist.

You have family connections in Alabama.

Yes, I have family connections in Alabama. My great-great (and between two and three more greats) grandfather was Menawa, or Monahwee as we spell it in Oklahoma. He and the Redsticks fought Andrew Jackson at the Battle of Horseshoe

Bend. He was later removed to Oklahoma, despite his attempts to keep his people in their homelands in what is now known as Alabama and Georgia. My cousin George Coser, Jr., says he's buried near Eufaula, Oklahoma, but recently I received an email from someone from Alabama, I believe, claiming descendency, who says Monahwee was buried in Kansas. Monahwee's story is a story I wish to pursue for a full-length feature film...This whole western hemisphere is Indian country. There are amazing stories that form our history, but so much has been told by those who flatten and stereotype anything Indian. Often those who stereotype are our own people.

Let's talk about your time at IAIA (the Institute of American Indians Arts in Santa Fe, NM), UNM (University of New Mexico in Albuquerque, NM) and the Iowa Writer's Workshop? How did you feel about the workshop? Have your feelings changed with distance?

This question could be a book; in fact, some of it will be. I'm currently working on a book of stories and many take place in those Indian school years, which was a time of great creative inspiration married with great despair. IAIA was an Indian boarding school run by the Bureau of Indian Affairs. In 1967 IAIA was a high school with a couple of years of postgraduate study. Students came from all over the U.S.—from Alaska, New York, Florida, everywhere. Many of us were from Oklahoma. We were all art majors from many different disciplines. I was there because of my artwork and at that time (my mother reminded me recently) I was drawing fashions. I had forgotten. She remembers that many of my designs later appeared in the fashion world. I had tapped into something. Later I became a drama and dance major and toured with one of the first all-native drama and dance troupes. I was one of the leads. This was a time (the late 1960s) of a tremendous awareness of ourselves as native peoples. We questioned...came to the conclusion that our cultural knowledge and exploration and creativity was our strength. And eventually I came to the conclusion, as did many others, that the wars within ourselves—whatever their source: colonization, the pressure of acculturation, and the ensuing family problems were our ultimate strength—made us allies.

To be accepted into the Iowa Writers Workshop was quite a coup, and I went because it was considered the best writers workshop in the country. I had applied to four graduate programs and all of them except Iowa had offered me some kind of assistance, including graduate assistantships, scholarships. I basically drove into Iowa City with two children and all that we owned in the back of a small Japanese-made truck, and the promise of some assistance from the EOP programs. We knew no one, and there was no visible Indian community. I was torn away from the familiar and in a vulnerable position so I'm sure that set my lens.

The first workshop the fall of 1976 was with a very well-known poet whose work I now admire. Then I didn't know her poetry; my catalogue of knowledge consisted nearly entirely of western U.S., non-European American, African, and Latin American poets. At UNM I was within eight hours of a BFA degree in Studio Art, painting and drawing. The poetry thing came later. Because of her I considered quitting, walking away in the first month of the workshop, so did Sandra Cisneros, a Mexican-American poet from Chicago. I was the only Indian.

Every week a worksheet of poems appeared in the English Department for each poetry workshop. The poems on the sheet were chosen from submissions from the respective classes. After nearly a month Sandra and I realized that neither of us had poems appear on the worksheet; we were the only ones in our class whose work had been ignored. We decided to approach the poet teaching our workshop together. We walked that sacred hall to her office, our sense of injustice making us brave. We knocked and stood at the door. At our appearance she flinched and made ready to run. We backed out. The next week we had work on the worksheets.

It became immediately obvious that I spoke a very different language, arrived in Iowa from a sensibility that was tribal, western, female and intuitive, a sensibility different than most of the other workshop participants. I envied their excellent educations, their long study of poetry, their confidence in their knowledge, their art. There was no place to comfortably fit in a literary canon that was male and white. For sustenance, several of us organized a Third World Writing Workshop. It included Sandra Cisneros; Kambone Obayani, an African-American novelist and horn player; Pam Durban, a Southern white woman writer; and Ricardo, from South Texas, who was the only workshop participant who wasn't in the writing workshop. He was a graduate student in the rhetoric program of the English Department. I also occasionally took part in a feminist writing workshop at the university's women's center. Other workshop students and faculty were inspiration and support, including Dennis Mathis, a brilliant fiction writer and painter; Jayne Anne Phillips, also in fiction; and Rosalyn Drexler, a playwright, painter, and novelist from New York who was once a visiting writer in the fiction program. I also spent most of my time the first year with the writers who were part of the International Writing Program. They included Leon Agusta, a poet from Indonesia; and Danarto, a playwright also from Indonesia. Being with them felt like home.

The workshop atmosphere was a struggle as I felt a stranger there. Later I compared notes with those who felt so much at the center of the program, were outspoken, lauded. I was surprised that they too expressed similar sentiments. We were all there to be writers and the workshop was a crucible, a shop to forge writers for a competitive writing world. We were linked in that struggle, that thirst for knowledge, for artistic brilliance...

The last semester of my two years there four of us were chosen to read our work to possible private funders for the workshop program. There were two men and two women, evenly divided between poetry and fiction. Jack Leggett introduced the writing program and then the student readers. I distinctly remember him emphasize that the program was primarily for male writers.

I am often asked by my writing students and by young writers around the country regarding my experience at Iowa because they are interested in attending. I always tell them that the workshop was a useful technical school, probably the best. I had to nourish my soul otherwise.

Who are the writers who have influenced you?

I would have to begin with singers first who drew attention to lyrics bound to music. They are Patsy Cline, Billie Holiday, and Nat King Cole. Also Bob Dylan, John Coltrane, Miles Davis, and Jim Pepper.

When I began writing it was first Simon Ortiz, the Acoma Pueblo poet; then Pablo Neruda, the Chilean poet; Leslie Marmon Silko; June Jordan; Adrienne Rich; especially Audre Lorde; and some African writers including Okot b'Pitek and Amos Tutuola. Also, Galway Kinnell. His *The Book of Nightmares* is brilliant and necessary. There are many others, too.

How do you define yourself as a writer?

I take that to mean, am I of a particular school, a particular persuasion? I am most often defined by others as: Native American, feminist, Western, Southwestern, primarily. I define myself as a human writer, poet and musician, a Mvskoke writer (etc)—-and I'm most definitely of the West, Southwest, Oklahoma and now my path includes Los Angeles and Honolulu...it throws the definition, skews it. It would be easier to be seen, I believe, if I fit into an easy category, as in for instance: The New York School, the Black Mountain School, the Beats— or even as in more recently, the Slam Poets. But I don't.

Do you have any particular discipline/writing routine?

It's often difficult given my erratic schedule. When I am on a deadline schedule I write in the morning, which will often lead into the afternoon. Otherwise it's usually morning, before the logical mind takes control, and then I work on music in the afternoon. The music usually has to wait because a saxophone is loud and everywhere I've lived has assured me a live audience—so I practice music in the afternoon, when most people are at work. Here in Honolulu I live on a slope that is dense with houses—sound travels. If I am too late getting to sax practice I assume that I am giving a concert, and will often pull out jazz standards and play a dinner show! The birds like it.

All this to say, that discipline is important. I believe Colette said, "Discipline is the key to freedom."

Talk about your publishing experiences—you've published chapbooks with small presses as well as an anthology with a major press...What are you currently working on? Do you have books in the pipeline?

My last three books were with Norton, a major publisher. My first book, *The Last Song,* was a chapbook from Puerto Del Sol Press, the next two, *What Moon Drove Me to This?* and *She Had Some Horses* were published by independent presses respectively, I. Reed Books (Ishmael Reed and Steve Cannon's imprint, no longer viable) and Thunder's Mouth Books (now a subsidiary of Avalon Books.) The next two were issued from university presses: *Secrets From the Center of the World*, the University of Arizona Press, and *In Mad Love and War*, Wesleyan University Press.

I've been lucky as all the publishers, from *She Had Some Horses* on, have kept the books in print. I did try to first publish both *Horses* and *Mad Love* with Norton but both were rejected, rather eloquently. The third manuscript I sent them, *The Woman Who Fell From the Sky*, was accepted. I have been publishing with them ever since. *How We Became Human: New and Selected Poems* was published in July 2002. A book of stories is forthcoming. I am also working on two new CD projects.

How does teaching influence writing?

I've taught intermittently since I graduated from Iowa. My first position was as an instructor at the Institute of American

Indian Arts, which was a two-year fine arts school. Its first incarnation was as a BIA boarding school turned into a fine arts high school, and is where I obtained my high school degree.

Later I did a few stints as an adjunct, then positions at the University of Colorado, Boulder and University of Arizona where I was tenured. Next I was a full tenured professor at the University of New Mexico, then left teaching for about six years. I wanted to concentrate on my music, and managed to make a living performing and writing. Winter quarter of 1998 I was a visiting writer at UCLA and then I taught again at UCLA this most recent fall and spring quarter, as a visiting professor in American Indian Studies and English.

Teaching can feed the writing; it can also be detrimental. What feeds me is the research for each class, each course and the interaction with students. Discipline and intuition walk together and can even engender flight. Detriment can occur with department and university-wide politics, with large classes and huge numbers of pages to read, with balancing the needs of teaching with your own work. Most of us who are teaching artists are always in the middle of creative projects, which is why we are hired in the first place.

The fall quarter [2002] begins in a few weeks. I just picked out the students for my workshop, based on their submitted manuscripts. Because the set of a boxed book with CD I wanted is not available, and I didn't find out until last week, I will now have to rethink the syllabus—actually, I think it will work out better. Having read the students' poems I can better surmise what each one needs, the poets' work that will challenge, resonate for each one...

In my workshops I stress the importance of reading and studying poetry, as well as the need for the practice of the art. Half the workshop is in discussion of the assigned readings. The other half discussion of students' own poetry. Technical development is crucial but isn't everything. If there's no soul, there's no poetry...

Talk about making the move from writing into music.

Poetry and music belong together—they came into the world together, they will leave together. If you want to get technical, then dance belongs as part of the equation. Every culture has a traditional base configured of poetry-music-dance, some of it secular, much of it sacred. Mvskoke philosophy can be gleaned from that base of such expression as can Greek, other European, African, all cultures.

At the Iowa Workshop, the prevailing rule was that to embellish a poem or poetry with emotive expression was to tarnish the expression of it, to get in the way of the words. This has metamorphed into the text-without-human-connection mode of thinking about poetry, about the making of literature. Sad, I think. It must be a lonely world, that world.

Adding saxophone is another thing—and I took up saxophone in my very late thirties. Like writing, it's a demanding discipline. Demands practice, study, and more practice. And faith, maybe faith is the prevalent force. And a love for the music, for the poetry, for the complexity of this strange and terrible place.

In 1989 I started with Keith Stoutenburg in Tucson. We put together a little combo. He was on guitar, keyboard, and voice, I played horn and spoke. We used the poems as a jumping off place. Later I hooked up with Susan Williams, and we brought in Zimbabwe Nkenya to play bass. Zimbabwe is a way-out, on-the-edge outside jazz player. With him we performed the first version of "Anna Mae" for a national NPR program. Then Susan's brother John moved to Albuquerque and we began Poetic Justice. Sometimes we'd work the music around the poems. Other times I'd bend the poems around the music, rewrite, add choruses, or a bridge. Since then I've written poems to go with particular vamps or melodies. Since, too, I've started another band, tentatively called "The Real Revolution."

What books do you recommend for young/novice writers?

I recommend that they read and hear poetry, from contemporary back through ancient times. That they listen to poetry, too, the poetry read from books, poetry performed, poetry that never finds its way in books. Most literature of the world isn't in books.

What books do you recommend for readers who may be unfamiliar with Native American writers/writing?

Where do I start? For fiction there's Leslie Marmon Silko, everything from her stories in the collection *Storyteller,* to *Ceremony,* to her latest, *Garden in the Dunes*; Greg Sarris, *Grand Avenue,* and *Watermelon Nights*; James Welch's novels; Louise Erdrich, especially *Love Medicine* and her most recent novel, and there are more that I will wish had come to me on this late Monday afternoon...For poetry, one of my favorite poets is Ray Young Bear, a Meskwaki poet; Simon Ortiz; there's Sherman Alexie who is a good poet, a better poet than fiction writer or screenwriter; I like Elizabeth Cook-Lynn's most recent book of poetry——that's a start...Roberta Whiteman is excellent, too.

Where do you see your career in ten years? Twenty years?

I feel like I'm just beginning to find my way to my best work. It's about process.

You've written "poetry is synonymous with truth telling." Would you care to elaborate?

The artists: the poets, musicians, painters, dancers make art from truth. Art that forges new paths, new insight, inspiration comes from the raw stuff floating in the connections between humans, animals, plants, stars, all life. Poets are the talk-singers, we find our art in the space between the words. There is where the truth lies.

I also consider the African griots, those whose poetry is shaped particularly to tell the truth, whatever the cost.

You've been described as a mystic...

The poet, too, can be a mystic, and I consider a mystic as one who sees beyond the obvious world, and moves accordingly. That is where my poetry has taken me and continues to lead me.

What do you believe/feel/know lies at the heart of your body of work?

Compassion. Joy.

Selected bibliography of Joy Harjo

Poetry:

The Last Song
What Moon Drove Me To This?
She Had Some Horses
Secrets from the Center of the World (Joy Harjo and Stephen Strom)
In Mad Love and War
The Woman Who Fell From the Sky
A Map to the New World
How We Became Human: New and Selected Poems: 1975-2001

CDs:

Letter From The End of the Twentieth Century
Native Joy for Real

Melinda Haynes

Melinda Haynes, the writer, is extraordinary. Her first two novels (*Mother of Pearl* and *Chalktown*) have sold more than 1.5 million copies. Her debut novel was an Oprah Book Club Selection and her work has garnered praise from critics, academics, readers, and her fellow writers. Sena Jeter Naslund wrote, "*Chalktown* is brilliant, completely original, transporting—Melinda Haynes is the new powerhouse writer of the South. Some day, people will say "Faulkner, O'Connor, Haynes."

Melinda Haynes, the interviewee, is equally extraordinary. She's compassionate, kind-hearted, open, funny, and empathetic. The tenderness in her characters seems to come from an equally tender spot in her.

Willem's Field, her last release, is her most accomplished and bravest novel to date.

Before you were a writer, you were a painter…

I did portrait work for seventeen years to help support my family. My clientele were from the Mobile/Spring Hill area (of Alabama). There came a time when it all came to be too much. Everything was due and my paintings were too gray. A client refused to pay for it and I went into a tailspin and quit. Just walked away. I realized I wanted to write.

How did you make the move from painting to writing?

I got a job at a small, local newspaper, *The Catholic Week*. I'm a Catholic convert. My father is a minister at a charismatic church. When I was growing up, my dad, who was a Baptist preacher, moved around with his churches and taught at Bible schools. There's great joy in the teachings of the Catholic Church and suffering is accepted as part of life.

My editor sent me to Jamaica to write about the poverty there. I spent five days in what felt like a garbage dump and just wrote about it. The story was called "Safe Distance."

A few days after I got back, Ray, the computer guy for the paper came by and said, "You write like a tall woman." He was the first to recognize what I wanted to do. When he stuck out his hand, I knew there was something special about him.

He's a retired Marine. He did three tours of duty in Vietnam. He has a degree in Computer Science. I started school at eighteen but married, dropped out, and had three daughters, by the time I was twenty-three. He's been my mentor in many ways. While he's all math and science, he has an appreciation for literature, an appreciation for the South, and in a larger way, an appreciation for the universal. On dates, he'd say, "Let's go to the library and check out some books."

While I didn't go to college, I love to learn. Other writers have been my teachers because I've been willing to hear other voices.

You married Ray...

When I met him and when I look at him, I know there is a God. The way I feel about Ray is in every book in some way.

Mother of Pearl **had its beginnings in your relationship with Ray.**

I started writing the novel as a Christmas gift for Ray. He found a section of it. I was 117 pages into it. He took the manuscript, without my knowledge, made a copy of it and found Wendy Weil. She's Alice Walker's agent and he knew I loved her work.

One Tuesday afternoon, at 4:30, I got a call at work from Wendy Weil. I was working with my daughter, who had the desk next to mine. She ran out into the hall to find Ray. Wendy agreed to represent me.

The second phone call I got about the book was from an editor. I didn't even know that editors buy books. We talked about the way the voice in the book was literary rather than commercial. Hyperion bought the novel that week.

I didn't write "commercially." Commercial success was never my goal. I only wanted to write in a way that pleased me.

Oprah chose *Mother of Pearl* as one of her Book Club Selections, which insured the novel's "commercial" success.

When Oprah called, I didn't know her voice or how she got my phone number because it was a private line. I told her the story of the book and the story of my life. It was a healing experience.

I didn't realize that having *Mother of Pearl* selected as part of the Book Club would be like winning the lottery and would allow me to do the one thing—writing—that I wanted to do most and what I wanted to do best.

Once the book hit, I felt amazement and disbelief. When my editor called to tell me about the additional printing and expanded book tour, I was terrified. I thought, "I CANNOT DO THIS." My husband worked with me, encouraging me to take one step and then, stand alone long enough to take another.

Chalktown [Haynes' second novel] was completed before Oprah called. While I felt suspended while I was writing *Mother of Pearl*, with *Chalktown*, I had a lower key experience. I felt like I said all I had to say and knew I couldn't think in terms of success. I felt more confident as a writer with each sentence.

The Oprah experience allowed me to not be burdened by debt, to pay for everything on a cash-only basis, and I can spend my time writing.

Where did the ideas for your books come from?

Every book started with an image from a dream. Then the characters start showing up, creating background music for the book.

Willem (from *Willem's Field*), came to me at a café in a restaurant in Little Rock, Arkansas. I was on a book tour, I was the fourth person reading, and I felt a panic attack coming on. [Haynes has agoraphobia.] I fainted and Steve Yarbrough, who wrote *The Oxygen Man*, came forward to help me. Considering the title of his book, the comedic side of me has always thought fate's choice of a rescuer ironic.

Afterwards, I couldn't face anybody. I didn't want to tell my agent or publisher. While I was sitting in this restaurant, I projected all I felt on to an older man sitting across from me. The image became very real for me. Some of the other characters who came along are parts of the puzzle.

Bruno, in part, was based on some of Ray's experiences in Vietnam. I did sit and watch footage from Ray's days in Vietnam and imagined what it was like for Leah to contemplate her marriage to Bruno. I loved following Leah and Bruno, watching their lives come together.

In the writing process, we're all the characters; and I am in every single character.

While you live in Alabama, your books have been set mostly in Mississippi...

All of the places we lived while I was growing up were in Mississippi and were places where dad had a church. The state has given me a warm reception.

Describe your workday.

I have coffee. I go to work. (Laughing) I'm more comfortable in the world of fiction than reality. It's such a comfort to do—see what they (the characters) are going to do and just write all day long.

I love the characters in my books. I like putting them in normal settings and seeing what happens. I hope I don't follow any stereotypes, and I try to create diversity.

What do you hope for when you write?

>Honesty.
>Truth.
>I want to touch the self.
>I want to grow with each book.
>Learning to listen.

Selected bibliography of Melinda Haynes

Fiction:

Mother of Pearl
Chalktown
Willem's Field

Roy Hoffman

Roy Hoffman's *Chicken Dreaming Corn*, an October 2004 BookSense pick, has been praised by Harper Lee as, "A story of great appeal in prose lean and clean." Other endorsements come from authors as diverse as Sena Jeter Naslund, Eli Evans, Albert Murray, Diane McWhorter, and Bill Aron. It has been widely reviewed, from *Southern Living* to the *Jewish Daily Forward*, from the *Boston Globe* and *Entertainment Weekly* to the *Jerusalem Post*.

Roy Hoffman is the author of *Almost Family*, winner of the Lillian Smith Award for fiction, and *Back Home: Journeys Through Mobile*. A native of Mobile, Alabama, he worked in New York City for twenty years as a journalist, speechwriter, editor, and teacher, before returning South as writer-in-residence at the *Mobile Register*, where he is now on staff. His essays and reviews have appeared in *The New York Times, Fortune, Southern Living*, and other publications.

How did you select the photograph for the book's dust jacket?

I found the photograph in the University of South Alabama's Archives in Mobile. It was one of several photos of shopkeepers on Dauphin Street. I didn't want to give the impression of the novel being a memoir by using a specific image of my grandfather. I liked the fact the shot told a little story of a small shop with its image of a shopkeeper on a certain date. The photograph is a touch later (the late 1940s) than the timeframe of the book. Designer Anne Richmond Boston added the fictional touches, changing the sign to M. Kleinman & Sons, the store at the heart of the novel.

Readers familiar with Mobile will recognize some of the names you've used. Were they meant as an inside joke? An homage?

I started writing the manuscript that became *Chicken Dreaming Corn* around 1992 while we were still living in New York. I wrote a version by hand on my lunch hours and just after work sitting in the shadow of the World Trade Center. Alabama was far away, and recalling names from my hometown's past was not only fun, but also helped ground my imagination in a familiar place. So there's a mix of actual and imagined names. No central character, however, is named for a real person. This technique of blending real with fictional names is inspired by works like *Ragtime*, but my real names aren't famous to anybody outside of Mobile. I also gave a nod to my New York neighborhood. The name Sahadi, which I use in the novel, is the name of a big Middle Eastern grocery store around the corner from where we lived in Brooklyn.

Even though *Chicken Dreaming Corn* is a novel, there are hints of autobiographical elements...

The book isn't a memoir and is only autobiographical in that a few stories have been passed down about as much in my previous novel, *Almost Family*.

I'd break down the sources of the novel as 20% research, 30% family stories, and 50% pure imagination. I certainly don't have a formula I work with. It's just the way my mind worked in this novel. Who knows how the next one will develop? I think it's important to direct the creative process, but not to control it. I enjoy drama too much to have written straight memoir in this case. By using third-person, I was able to spend time alone with my characters and that was aesthetically pleasurable, particularly concerning Morris.

I also enjoyed the process of shifting the point of view in the novel among different characters, especially between Morris and Pablo Pastor, the Cuban cigar maker. I imagined what it was like for my own grandfather in his daily world. By writing the book as fiction I got to dress the characters in their costumes, enter their memories, be with them behind closed doors.

You're both Southern and Jewish and blend elements from both traditions in your writing. Do you find your psyche is dominated by either tradition?

Spiritually and philosophically I'm Jewish. Culturally, in terms of what reverberates from my childhood, I'm very much Southern. I don't see a contradiction in that. After all, Mexican Jews pray on the Sabbath and enjoy mariachi music. I believe in the tenets of Judaism, celebrate the religious holidays, and feel an empathy with Jews worldwide; yet I enjoy blues music and bar-b-cue. (I don't keep kosher.) Having grown up on Alabama's coast, I feel at home sitting on a wharf on Mobile Bay with a cold drink watching the sunset. There's even a photograph of me on the dock in Bill Aron's photo album of the Jewish South, *Shalom, Y'all.*

Religiously, I'm observant, but hardly strict. I served on the board of trustees of my Reform Jewish congregation, Springhill Avenue Temple in Mobile, and the bat mitzvah of my daughter, Meredith, with my wife, Nancy, and Dad alongside her, was one of the most moving events of my life.

I come from an Orthodox background on my father's side, so the characters and their religious sensibilities I write about in *Chicken Dreaming Corn* are not unfamiliar. My dad, Charles, who continues to be a monumental influence on me, was born in 1909. He's 95, and still practices law in Mobile. I highlighted him in a photo-essay I wrote the text for in *Fortune* magazine, "Working Past 90." Having grown up over his parents' store, he keeps the Mobile of yesteryear—the immigrant crossroads of the Southern seaport—colorful and vivid. His father was born in 1881, so I'm getting stories originating 120 years ago handed directly on to me.

There were other family members on my father's side who, fleeing Eastern Europe, ended up in Argentina. I'll never forget being in high school and having our South American relatives visit us in Alabama. The only language the old-timers had in common was Yiddish, the international language of the Jews.

My father's family influenced *Chicken Dreaming Corn* while my mother's family influenced *Almost Family*.

Mobile is one of the most traditionally multi-ethnic, multi-cultural cities in the South because it is a seaport...

In my novel, within a few pages, you can find Southern drawls, Yiddish, Hebrew, and Spanish. And there's some Greek, of course. Perhaps the "new" Southern novel, which I hope mine to be—even though it's set back in time—is, at its core, profoundly American. By that I mean that the South is not seen as isolated and apart, but coursed-through with cultures and influences from around the world. Those cultures may seem hidden, at first. But one of my interests as a writer of both fiction and non-fiction is to shine light on characters who may have stood in the shadows before.

You're on the regular visiting faculty at Spalding's Brief Residency MFA program in Louisville, Kentucky. What's the experience like for you?

I love teaching, both in delving into the creative process of students, and in the fellowship with my colleagues. Since we are "in residence" at Spalding only ten days in October, and ten in May, there's an intensity to the workshop experiences. The immersion in pure literary activity for that short period of time - including faculty and student readings, panel discussions, and constant dialogue over meals and nightcaps—is exhilarating, rejuvenating.

The rest of the term is demanding in a different way. Each teacher works as a mentor with five students who send us packets of material for critique. I mentor in both fiction and creative non-fiction. Our MFA director, Sena Jeter Naslund, author of the novels *Ahab's Wife* and *Four Spirits,*, emphasizes that, as mentors, we meet the students on their own levels. The program is positive, supportive, nurturing.

One of the things I relish about writing is always being open to surprise. That certainly was true in my early drafts of *Chicken Dreaming Corn*, where I wasn't sure who might walk into Morris's store next. You never know what's around the corner, and maybe you make the discovery while jotting in your notebook, or writing poetry just for yourself.

There's a similar experience in working as a journalist, but it's out in the world, not only inside one's head. Being a staff writer for my hometown newspaper, *The Mobile Register*, means making those discoveries on the street—having the freedom to go where I need for the story, and the license to talk to anyone who'll talk to me. It's a great way to find the seeds of imaginative stories, too.

Selected bibliography of Roy Hoffman

Fiction:

Almost Family
Chicken Dreaming Corn

Non-fiction:

Back Home: Journeys Through Mobile

Sheri Joseph

Sheri Joseph's debut cycle of stories, *Bear Me Safely Over,* has earned favorable reviews and the praise of critics.

Joseph, who earned her PhD at the University of Georgia, joined the faculty as an Assistant Professor of English and Creative Writing at Georgia State University, where she teaches both graduate and undergraduate fiction writing courses.

Her short fiction appeared in several literary journals including: *The Georgia Review, Shenandoah, Virginia Quarterly Review, Other Voices,* and *Kenyon Review.* "The Elixir," which is included in *Bear Me Safely Over,* was a finalist for the National Magazine Award. She has been a fellow at the Bread Loaf and Sewanee Writers' Conferences, and at the MacDowell Colony.

Where did you grow up? Where were you educated? And where do you live/teach now?

I grew up mostly in the Memphis area and attended the University of the South, a small liberal arts college in east Tennessee. After graduation, I lived in Georgia, in the areas where the book is set, for about twelve years…most of that was graduate school in Athens, where I did the writing.

Now, after a brief loop into Kentucky, I'm lucky enough to have returned to a job in what feels like my home state, especially because I'm connected to it through my writing. This fall I started teaching in the creative writing program at Georgia State University, which is such an exciting program. I can't quite believe I'm here. By coincidence, I've been writing a book set in Atlanta for the past year, so I get a charge out of walking to my classes through downtown, feeling that I'm at the center of my own fictional world as well as a real city with so much happening.

Was *Bear Me Safely Over* your dissertation?

Bear Me Safely Over was actually the book I wrote immediately after my dissertation, a novel. I grappled with that book for about eight years, seriously, and was never able to make it work to my own satisfaction. But I learned so much from the process of drafting and redrafting and especially restructuring, and all the while, I think *Bear Me Safely Over* was coming together somewhere else in my head. So when I sat down with this second book, which is actually a cycle of stories, it came much more easily and naturally than the novel.

Jim Kilgo at Georgia was my mentor through both books, and he was the one who believed in my work and gave me the confidence to get through the shaky spots. He was wonderful at reading my work and explaining what I was doing with it, which helped authenticate it for me. He read the first full draft of *Bear Me Safely Over* in one night, and the next night, which was the night of his own book signing for *Daughter of My People,* he took me aside and told me, "THIS is your book." Stan Lindberg, the late editor of *The Georgia Review*, published my first story ("The Elixir," the last story in the book), and that was another invaluable boost of confidence.

Who were/are your literary influences?

The writers who I've spent the most time with, and who I hope have taught me something are Shakespeare, William Faulkner, and Toni Morrison. Marilynne Robinson's novel, *Housekeeping*, made a big impression on me, as did Louise Erdrich's *Love Medicine*, from which I borrowed the structural principles for this book. There's a little nod in the book to Sherwood Anderson…and so many of my favorite writers have written [story] cycles——Ernest Hemingway, Jean Toomer, Eudora Welty, Katherine Ann Porter.

Talk about the book's structure.

Though a lot of people seem to be reading this book as a novel and finding it works that way, I've always seen it as a cycle of stories. The form helps explain the fact that the book moves from first to third person, past tense to present, and jumps around in time and place, exploring different lives connected to the two central families. Individually, the stories stand alone, and most appeared previously in literary journals. But the connections among them are all intentional, part of the original design of the book.

How did the collection originate?

I started this book with two incidents from a summer when I was working as a stall mucker at a riding stable...rather small events that seemed to want a place in fiction. One was that I got kicked in the middle of the back by a horse (and that's hard to do!). The other is that I started finding live hummingbirds on the barn floor...the first one I accidentally kicked across the floor before I knew what it was.

Those two kicking incidents frame the book, and I started by giving them to characters very different from myself, people at the right moment in their lives to be affected by them more deeply than I could be. The story of the two families came out of the characters involved in each incident—Curtis and Florie. Sidra, who is Florie's surviving daughter and Curtis's fiancé becomes the bridge between the two.

Then Paul, who more or less takes over the book, came out of a rancorous reference in Curtis's story...I intended to give Paul a chance to respond, but then he wouldn't shut up.

Florie lost a daughter to AIDS and Paul is gay...with AIDS, I wanted the threat of homophobia and violence to be present, something Paul would have to acknowledge and contend with, but also not so overwhelming as to turn him into a martyr. I didn't want to simplify his life that way, or even with a story like "Rest Stop," in which Paul is faced directly with his community's hatred, to let that social/political issue become the center.

It's more about Paul's relationship with his father and stepmother, his struggle to live up to their expectations and also find a way to be honest about who he is. Without much guidance, he's searching for a place in the world where he fits, and that leads him in some dangerous directions. But he's strong and resourceful and probably just plain lucky enough to survive the trip.

Did you set out to explore the new American family?

Those themes are definitely present in the book, though "the new American family" sounds loftier than anything I was intentionally aiming for! I write about particular connections between people—the lives of my characters as I see them—and hope that something more universal comes through. I tend to see people in patterns of connectedness, and for my central characters (here Sidra and Paul) the struggle is usually between individual desires and a sense of responsibility to others. As people betray or leave behind or fail in their original connections, especially to biological family, they find replacements in other people, often awkward replacements—not just stepfamilies, but friends substituted for siblings, lovers serving as absent fathers, the children of strangers replacing one's own. And maybe that's the new American family—no longer that ideal family unit, but something more haphazard and organic, formed out of loss and guilt and a deep desire to do better the next time.

Is there any chance you'll write a sequel?

I don't think of it as a sequel, but the book I'm writing now, a novel, involves the later lives of two of the characters, Paul and Kent. I'm not sure whether it's wise to remain caught up with this material, but I don't seem to have a choice—I just have a lot more to say about them. Though *Bear Me Safely Over* leaves them on a fairly positive note, their reality is obviously a lot more troubled and complicated, and I'm drawn to continue exploring that. I won't say too much about it, except that the novel-in-progress begins four years later and in a very different context. There are some new characters who take major steering roles. I hope there will be some readers out there who love these characters as much as I do, enough to want to spend more time with them. But I also intend the new book to stand on its own and inhabit its own territory.

Where do you hope your career will be in ten years? Twenty years?

That's a hard one. For years, all I've wanted is a life that will allow me the time to write, and a publisher who believes in my work enough to print it, however weird it is—and it seems I might have that now...I really hope I can be the kind of writer whose books other writers and book people will read, love, remember, and keep on their shelves. I can't imagine ever being well-known...And, I'd like to have students who say that I've helped them become better writers.

Selected bibliography of Sheri Joseph

Fiction:

Bear Me Safely Over

Catherine Landis

Catherine Landis possesses the rare gift of balance. A fine novelist—her works have been praised for their intelligence, compassion, and grace—she also worked in the last presidential campaign and volunteers in her community. A wife and mother, she protects her family's privacy, separating herself from her writer's persona.

Her conversation, like her novels, *Some Days There's Pie* and *Harvest*, is articulate, thoughtful, smart, sensible, and sensitive. Dedicated to her craft, Landis creates characters reminiscent of long-lost family members and friends. If, as Landis says, writing is "like making soup," reading her writing is like eating a good soup in that the reader feels nourished and satisfied afterwards.

Where are you from?

I was born in Birmingham. We only lived there two years. I grew up in Chattanooga. After college, I lived several places. I followed my husband while he was finding a permanent job. We lived in eastern North Carolina; Lexington, Kentucky; and Augusta, Georgia. We've lived in Knoxville for the last seventeen years. It's "home."

Where did you attend college?

I was in the second graduating class of women at Davidson College in North Carolina. I was also the first woman editor of the college newspaper. I thought nothing about it. We were young and it was "just what we did." There had never been women…I sort of forgot we were groundbreaking. We felt so welcomed. We assimilated easily.

The professors treated us as if they could not wait to have us there.

Talk about writing with historical sources.

I'm not the best researcher and it's not the most fun for me. In school, I was always the student who got more from the teachers than the books.

I was helped more by talking to people, than what I read at the library.

Tennessee Valley Authority's Ted Nelson made the books come alive for me. He was also able to give me these books of reports written by TVA relocation workers. I did not want to use the story of any one person; I simply used them to get a flavor of what their lives were like. One of the people interviewed used the phrase, "another THINK coming," which was something my grandmother, who was from Texas, said. It sounded so right for the book. I was glad to know that people in Appalachia used the phrase as well.

Some of the people interviewed were not unhappy about moving.

A friend with lots of relatives told me stories about women who could douse waters and who claimed to heal burns or the thrush in a baby's mouth. Somebody in her family burned up when the dress she was wearing caught fire.

Writing is like making soup. You throw it all in and make something new.

When I was writing, people would ask, "What is your book about?" All I had to do was mention the influence or impact of TVA and people would grab me with breathless urgency. They told me, "I hope you've told my story." The idea has a deeply personal resonance. I had no idea. None.

When I started the book, my whole focus was Leda and Daniel, but the story was not complete until I added Arliss and gave him a voice.

In researching, I read more than I could put in the book. There's so much more to be written about the time when TVA was building all the dams. Back then, there were two schools of thought about what they were doing, some having a more Utopian vision for social change, and others simply wanting to tame the rivers. I don't think we've finished that argument in this country even today.

What is the significance of place in your work?

At the Southern Festival of Books, I was on a panel with five other writers and our topic was place. I started laughing because everything is place.

One of the themes in both your novels seems to be change or upward mobility...

I've never thought about the similarities and differences. They came about so differently.

With *Harvest*, I was writing about how people deal with change, the effects of change.

I've thought a great deal about the differences in class, how people are judged by class. Who they are. What they do. The ways they try to get away from their class and strive to cover up their background and the heartache that comes with that. Class is a fact of life...there's an inherent unfairness.

Ruth (from *Some Days There's Pie*) and Daniel (from *Harvest*) both try to get away from their class. Daniel is ashamed of who he was. Daniel never seems to learn. He got right into his life...moved into the upper class around nine.

Ruth was always left out, never assimilated.

Daniel got there and stayed there. He betrayed allegiances.

Is there any chance you'll write a sequel to *Harvest?*

It took a long time to write *Harvest,* four or five years. I was trying hard to make the characters become real people rather than using the characters to move the plot along.

When I close the book, I'm done. It's so nice when readers embrace characters. But the world becomes totally different and I can't go back there again.

I did have an image of Leda parking outside a house where they clearly used to live. In the image, Leda and Susan are older women driving back into the subdivision of what used to be the farm. They are remembering. Andy and Hannah have grown up. Hannah's a doctor…

How do you feel about the Appalachian label?

Harvest was nominated for Appalachian Book of the year and certainly my work in *Harvest* deals with the land . . .

Some Days There's Pie I would consider more Southern than Appalachian, and that would hold true for my third book.

Who are your favorite authors?

Besides Shakespeare? Right now, there's Jose Saramago, the Portuguese novelist who won the Nobel Prize. I love the craft of Ian McEwan and Carol Shields.

I read a ton of non-fiction. I have about twenty books in my pile.

I loved Wendell Berry's *The Wild Birds* and Bailey White's short stories. She's a complete master. Her work knocks me out…There are so many books I could just go on and on…

What's your next book?

It's going to deal with the injustice of the judicial system…There's a strong woman protagonist with a strong voice. She's educated. She's a high school librarian. Librarians of the world can rejoice. She's a hero.

What would you still like to be asked or like to say about writing?

Just that I like to hone back into this notion that writing, to me, has no shortcuts. It can be an extremely frustrating endeavor. It can be lonely. The exhilaration I feel when I have an idea…when I can convey an idea through language, is unlike any experience in life. Writing takes dogged persistence.

What's your idea of the perfect day?

I'm pretty simple. I'd probably go ahead and get up early—we'd be on the beach—I'd take a long run. I love to work so there would be work to do. I'd have dinner with my family—my children, my husband, and my parents. Then we'd play cards and go outside to look at the stars. I'd end the day by reading until I had to go to bed.

Selected bibliography of Catherine Landis

Fiction:

Some Days There's Pie
Harvest

Jill McCorkle

Only twenty-six when she started publishing, Jill McCorkle's many long-time readers may feel as if they've "grown up" with her. Her five novels, *July 7th, The Cheerleader, Tending to Virginia, Ferris Beach,* and *Carolina Moon,* encompass the many varieties of Southern womanhood. Her three collections of short stories, *Crash Diet, Final Vinyl Days,* and *Creatures of Habit,* have balanced the themes of change and acceptance with a deft wit and graceful writing. It's hard to imagine contemporary writing or Southern writing without her influence.

Jill McCorkle was inducted into the Fellowship of Southern Writers in April 2003 alongside authors Madison Smartt Bell, Kaye Gibbons, Barry Hannah, Yosef Komunyakka, John Shelton Reed, Ellen Bryant Voight, and Allen Weir.

Where do you live and teach now?

I live near Boston...I am permanently on the faculty of the Bennington College MFA in Writing Program—It's a low-residency program so much of the work is done by mail. I also have recently taught at Brandeis University.

Do you still consider yourself to be a Southerner and a Southern writer?

I absolutely consider myself both a Southerner and a Southern writer. All I have to do is open my mouth for people to know I'm from the South. Though I've lived here over ten years, I have not lost my accent—AND I have not lost my love and desire for the South. My work is steeped in the Southern landscape I knew growing up—southeastern North Carolina—the food and foliage, the language. I rely heavily on childhood influences in my writing, particularly that of the desire to tell a story or to be told a story. I think that a strong sense of place and an emphasis on storytelling are two major components of Southern writing.

Do you have a favorite of the books you've written?

Picking favorites is always a hard thing because they all represent a certain stage of life. I don't think you'd ever write the same book twice because of that passage of time. Still, I have those books I feel closest to and perhaps most proud of technically. I feel close to *Tending to Virginia* because the novel was inspired heavily by the voices of my grandmother and my great-aunt. For me the novel was a kind of love song written to those generations before us, the ones whose stories have formed our histories. If I were asked to pick one novel, I might say *Carolina Moon*. I'm not sure if this is because it's the most recent novel or because it was the culmination of lots of years. It was a novel I started and then wasn't sure where to go so I stopped and wrote another book. I did that twice before actually writing it and so the characters Denny and Quee and Tom were characters who were already up and moving around years before the book began. As for stories, I'd say *Creatures of Habit*—it's the most recent and it's the collection I felt most confident about.

How do you juggle parenting, writing, and teaching?

I have two children. It is a constant juggling act especially since I have had only one semester during the past 15 years when I wasn't teaching at all. And this ties in with the next question as well. I used to have a schedule—pre-family—I got up and wrote from 5 to 8 every day then went to work. I realized when my daughter was born, that I would not be able to keep that schedule but instead needed to be flexible. So I write when I can. I try to clear out nice big blocks of time during the school day or when I can steal away for a day or two, but most of the time I am engaging in what you call a more impressionistic manner. I take lots and lots of notes. I save and store until I get a big block of time and/or it feels like the top of my head will fly off—whichever comes first! I plan a little with my work—I usually have a vague idea of my direction, but I have also learned to leave myself open to surprises and turns I did not expect. It's a disaster to force work to stay on course, I think—there is much to be gained by hitting a rhythm and being true to THAT instead of an original plan.

Writing short stories was a slight departure for you and *Creatures of Habit* received almost universally good reviews. Is the short story form more difficult to work in than the novel form for you?

I was very proud of *Creatures* and the reviews it got. The reviews reassured me and made me feel eager to write more stories. I began as a novelist, but always kept coming back to the story. I wanted to feel that I could work within the form and I felt most confident within the pieces in *Creatures*.

I have found stories to be more difficult than novels. I'm sure other writers would say the opposite. And yet, I'm drawn to the challenge of the story form. I'm also drawn to poetry, yet have had no success there. Usually what I dabble with in poetry finds its way into sentences and paragraphs. The experimentation is wonderful for attention to rhythm and word choice and I always encourage students to try poetry—both reading and writing.

Who were your writing teachers?

I was very lucky when it came to writing teachers as I think I had some of the very best. Max Steele, Lee Smith, Louis Rubin were my teachers at University of North Carolina, and then Richard Dillard and Rosanne Coggeshall at Hollins with George Garrett as a visiting writer. I would also list in that line-up my editor (could that be? Yes, since '84) Shannon Ravenel—I never work on a book that I don't come away feeling I have learned something. Shannon is a wonderful teacher as well as editor. I think that there are some aspects of creative writing that can be taught. I often compare it to teaching any sport or art. Here are the basics. You can learn them. This is how you stand at home plate. This is how you hold the bat. This is what you're looking for in a pitch, and so on. You can teach all of that. What the batter has to find within himself is the sense of timing and movement that enables him to hit the ball and then once it's hit to follow through, to run, etc. So there's a lot you can teach— the rest is all about encouraging the individual to tap his or her own resources.

What has it been like having your work included in the University of South Carolina's Understanding Contemporary Writers Series?

I feel flattered, of course, to see a book written about my work. I was flattered that someone of Barb Bennett's intelligence and talent had spent so much time with my work! Sometimes I read articles where my work is discussed and I feel that I'm reading about someone else. I'm thinking, Did I do that? When I'm writing, I never think beyond the scene I'm in at the moment. I think too much thinking for a writer can be a terrible thing. I don't want to think beyond what my characters are thinking, at least not until revision when I have assumed a different stance. For me the goal is always one of seeking reality and a kind of emotional truth.

What's your next project?

I'm working on a novel that is taking me longer than I thought it would—it's just one that has needed lots of percolating time. So, I've written a few stories here and there in between. I always have a project. Usually I have several…My greatest fear is to find myself without one!

What do you see as the "theme" of your writing?

I'm intrigued by the way many writers feel they write the same story again and again. I do. I feel I am always writing about acceptance. To me, a character who finds a way to accept what life has placed before him has found the resolution. So again and again, I am putting characters out there in a situation that is not ideal and hoping that they can find something to hold onto via acceptance. To me that is a happy ending.

What was the best day of your life?

Other than the obvious one? The births of my children and there are those obvious childhood memories that forever serve as my springboard into both fiction and life. I look to those moments in my writing life. One day that I will never forget is the day that the *Daily Tarheel* (the campus paper) reviewed the campus literary magazine (*The Cellar Door*) and the review focused on my story, which was also my first published story. I was sitting in the student union and read a sentence that began: "Clearly this issue's biggest success is…" and then the reviewer went on to describe my story. It seems I levitated and did not come down for weeks. When I got to the apartment I rented with my best friend from high school, she had cut out the article, highlighted all the parts about me and taped it on the door. We spent the rest of the day celebrating and talking about what we planned to do with our lives. It was one of those perfect times when it seemed life would always be that way and would go on forever.

Selected bibliography of Jill McCorkle

Fiction:

July 7th
Creatures of Habit
Carolina Moon
Crash Diet
Ferris Beach
The Cheerleader
Final Vinyl Days
Tending to Virginia

Jackson Tippett McCrae

Jackson Tippett McCrae is a novelist with an unusual flair for blending research with storytelling. Educated at the University of Alabama, the University of North Texas, and The Juilliard School in New York, McCrae draws on a diverse background of art, music, and dance, and incorporates these elements into his novels and short stories.

What were your literary influences in researching *The Bark of the Dogwood?*

I read Keller's *The Story of My Life* a couple of times, along with all of Capote's works, and the biography of Capote by Gerald Clarke. Also Plimpton's book on Capote. I read the biographies of Carson McCullers (Carr), Thomas Wolfe (Donald), and used as a reference book *Helen and Teacher* by Joseph Lash. I read again all the Southern literature I could find, having been through most of it already in high school. All of the Tennessee Williams, McCullers, and almost all Faulkner. I was trying to glean the Southern writer's experience and what it was like for them to go North and then come back home, as did Wolfe and McCullers.

Talk about the novel's structure and the writing process.

I initially wrote the first draft of the book in three weeks, while working a full-time job. The thing just came out. Then the book sat around for several years and I did nothing to it. I dug it out when I left my last job in publishing and began revising it. I'd say I spent about a solid year on research, but in reality it was my entire lifetime since I'm from that area and things tend to stay with you.

After I had the main part of the book written, I made a physical representation of each chapter in the book on enormous cards, indicating what was happening and then refining it so that things flowed naturally and hooked into one another. I wanted to get a bird's-eye view of the thing, to make sure the climax came at a certain point and that certain themes and ideas were spaced out visually.

By the time I had finished, I had re-written the book fifteen times from beginning to end. I don't mean edited. I mean totally rewritten it. I also did a "date" grid, showing who was born, where and when. I even did each character's Zodiac signs to determine some of the traits they would have.

Then there was the research on cultural events, to determine if they fit into the time line. I had to make sure the Julia Child show was on the air in a certain year, or that a movie with Elizabeth Taylor had been released within a certain time frame. Then there was the research on the gun that was used to kill the mother. Little things like that, they all added up and took a great deal of time.

You used a story within a story framework with alternating voices...

I'm guessing you mean the fact that the "stories" are written in first person, encompassing one style, and the other chapters are in a different style. I did this for several reasons. I like playing with styles, since I feel comfortable writing in many different ones, and I thought that the alternation of voices made the novel more dimensional.

Also, I had done some research on multiply personality disorder and DID (Dissociate Identity Disorder) and worked that into the book. It's probably not obvious to anyone but me, but Strekfus, the main character, is supposed to have a split personality or at least some type of personality disorder. Most persons who have this have suffered a traumatic event, especially early in life, and, when you get to chapter 28, then you know what I'm talking about. So, he's actually the one writing the book, and as a result, writes in two voices and two styles (if not more). Readers may have also noticed that there is not a single sex scene in the book. I don't consider chapter 28 to be a sex scene as rape, to me, is violence. There is a very brief mention of some neighbors having sex, but nothing too graphic. I felt that Strekfus was a rather sexless character, having been damaged by his early experiences. You may have noticed that nowhere in the book does it mention a love interest, hetero-or homosexual-wise.

Strekfus's father is a cold individual who rarely, if ever, shows his son any outward signs of affection.

I felt that if I was going to show the father as being the monster that he was, that I had better explain how he got that way. Hence, the tracing back through the generations to show how his father was, etc. I didn't feel that you could have this man performing this heinous deed and not explain how he got so deranged in the first place. Strekfus talks, early on in the book, about wanting to stop the cycle of abuse; therefore never planning to have children.

Explain the Helen Keller references and epigrams throughout the novel.

While the epigrams sometimes comment literally on the action, at other times they're sarcastic or ironic. These were taken, for the most part, out of context from the original, and used by Strekfus as he sees fit. It is just another example of his identifying with Keller as he identified with the maid, Althea. He felt trapped, persecuted, blind, deaf, dumb, abused, and just about everything else that a minority or handicapped person experiences.

Young Strekfus is brilliant. Once of his earliest memories is of reading the encyclopedia and learning the Latin names for plants, a habit that certainly sets him apart from the other children in Infanta, Alabama.

Again, I did research on personality disorders for the book, one of them being a disorder called Hyperlexia. With this disorder, children learn to read and write by the age of three or four, and usually have an enormous vocabulary. But they often have no social skills. So far, the study of this disorder has shown that the children usually suffered a traumatic event while very young. The disorder wasn't known at the time Strekfus would have been a child, and so I didn't mention it, but it was in the back of my mind while writing his character. Also, the Latin names have a special significance as he later argues with the housekeeper over their use. They have made a pact that he will teach her Latin names and she will teach him the common ones so that he can, "call things by their rightful names." He never holds up his end of the bargain in the story, that is, not until the very end when he titles the book *The Bark of the Dogwood*—instead of *The Bark of the Cornus florida*. It's the ultimate homage, in his mind, to the woman who saved him.

Why did you use references to Truman Capote throughout the book?

Capote was selected for several reasons. I've always liked his style for one thing. For another, Strekfus fancies himself to be like Capote, so much so, that he tries to copy some of the author's style and even makes reference to a short story that Capote wrote titled "Children on Their Birthdays." In the Capote story, he starts out by saying, "Yesterday afternoon, the six-o'clock bus ran over Miss Bobbit." This parallels the opening of chapter 20 where the bus runs over Brad Castratis (an anagram, by the way, for "racist bastard"). Then there is the fact that Strekfus was named after a playmate his father had in New Orleans. Truman Capote spent some time in New Orleans at the same time Srekfus's father was there.

Several people have commented on the main character's name being very un-Southern. I did a huge amount of research on this. "Strekfus" actually comes from Truman Capote's real name—Truman Streckfus Persons. His father named him this after a steamboat that ran from New Orleans, up and down the

Mississippi. Beltzenschmit is a bastardization of a Civil War General's name, Beltzhoover.

Did you choose Keller and Capote because they made lives outside of the South and didn't look back?

I'm not sure I agree with the idea that Keller and Capote both left the South without looking back. I think anyone who has lived in the South can never escape. It's such a potent environment and culture that even a short while there seems to alter the person. Certainly Capote carried it with him all his life. His most important works, other than *In Cold Blood*, were *Other Voices, Other Rooms* and *The Grass Harp* (in my opinion), both of which look back on his youth and the South. Even *Breakfast at Tiffany's* has a pull back to Texas (the South to some people). I know that Helen Keller ended up in Connecticut, actually a little down the road from where I live now. Talk about ironic. And by the way, "Yes," I was actually locked inside Helen Keller's home. My entire family was, but I thought it a more dramatic setting to only have Strekfus incarcerated.

Where are you from?

I was born in Alabama and grew up there. I attended the University of Alabama for about a year and a half, and then transferred to the University of North Texas. Then moved to New York and attended the Juilliard School. Certainly my experiences in these places colored the book and I set much of it in Alabama and Texas. And New York.

Is any of the novel autobiographical?

While I drew on some actual incidents that happened to me, for the most part, the novel is fiction. I have this theory that if you set out to write strictly the truth, some fiction will creep in, and if you set out to write strictly fiction, some truth will get in the thing. Look at history. Look at the Bible.

How long have you lived away from the South?

I moved to New York in the '80s, then to Connecticut a few years ago. I don't actually consider New York City to be part of the "North" so it never bothered me to live there. New York is a thing in itself and is such a conglomerate of cultures that I didn't feel that North-South friction much. Connecticut was a different story. I actually had great anxiety about living in a Yankee state. I've gotten over it since it tends to look a lot like Alabama. Plus, it allows me easy access to New York. I do miss the South, though.

When you were writing the novel, did you think in terms of Southern Gothicism?

I just sat down at the keyboard and let loose. I totally let myself go and let the characters do what they wanted. I was quite shocked by what some of them did. I had some ideas about what I wanted to do, but as anyone (who is any good) will tell you, if you try to control the thing too much it comes out stilted. I went back later and molded the work and looked at the form, but for me, to start out with an outline and a completed structure first off, is death. It may work for some people, but not me. I want the writing to be organic, and if that means it takes me someplace that's uncomfortable, then so be it. I was told by several story analysts who read the book that it had to be this or that—Gothic, horror, biography, humor, etc. I ignored them. I'm glad I did. I didn't want to write something that was like anyone else's work. There's a good hint to this in one of the opening chapters where Strekfus is given an aptitude test and he has to match up several objects. He doesn't do it as a "normal" person would and this is a major key to the structure and style of the novel.

What's your next project?

I've finished a collection of short stories titled *The Children's Corner*. Some are set in the South, some in Connecticut, New York, New Jersey, and other locations. The longest story in the book is a novella set in Lawrence County, Alabama. I think it's my favorite of all my writings to date. It's about a woman who has Alzheimer's and is in a nursing home. My second full-length novel is now published—*Katzenjammer: Soon to be a Major Motion Picture.*

Selected bibliography of Jackson Tippett McCrae

Fiction:

The Bark of the Dogwood—A Tour of Southern Homes and Gardens
The Children's Corner
Katzenjammer: Soon to be a Major Motion Picture

Joan Medlicott

After two other careers, Joan Medlicott fell in love with writing. Readers have fallen in love with Medlicott's "Covington Ladies" series of novels about three women of "a certain age" spreading their wings and forging new lives for themselves.

When and how did you start writing?

I co-authored a non-fiction book called *Celibate Wives: Breaking the Silence,* back in 1992, and fell in love with writing, but did not like non-fiction. I started writing a novel without any idea what I was doing, or how to do it. I was without doubt the worse member of any writing group and I loved it so much I was determined to learn. I never allowed criticism to dissuade me. I took classes, read and read books, took workshops and began to learn and grow. I hope I always will learn and grow. I was sixty-four when I began *The Ladies of Covington.*

What did you do before you were a writer?

I have a BA in history, and an MC in Counseling. I have been the Director of the Division of Beautification for the Virgin Islands Government. Horticulture, you might call it, and then, after moving to Boca Raton, Florida, I developed all kinds of programs (not computer!) in-house and for the community of The Mae Volen Senior Center in Boca Raton, where I lived for fifteen years. Writing is my third and well-loved career. It came as a gift from God and I am forever grateful.

Talk about your experiences with finding a publisher.

To find a pub, there are rules of the game: when your novel or non-fiction book is ready to be sent out, you want to get a book on how to write a query letter and follow instructions.

Then go to the library or buy a book—*Writers Market*, which lists agents and their preferences. Choose about twenty-five, send them the query letter and remember to enclose a post card with your name and address and stamp on one side and on the other three boxes you make. After a box it says "Please send…pages of your novel," Box 2. "Please send me the entire novel," Box 3, "I am not interested." That way an agent can check what she or he wants and you get an answer in a reasonable time. Otherwise you can wait for a very long time.

Have you been surprised by your success and your sales?

Yes, and grateful.

Is there any autobiography in your writing?

Bits and pieces, things that happen to me or to friends or others I know find their way into the novels, but it [the book] is not autobiographical in any sense.

Would you like to talk about your personal life?

My husband and I are married thirty-five years this June—a second marriage for both of us, and we blended a family of six kids—three his, three mine. We have seven grandchildren. Most of our kids live between Atlanta and Raleigh, North Carolina, and one in Florida, so we see them regularly, which is great.

Are there any more "Covington Ladies" novels in the works?

Novel number four is already finished and novel number five is half done. There's no title yet for book four. That seems to be one of the last things that happen when the publisher is the one coming up with the name. I have two other novels, not yet published, but they will be in a year or so. One is set in Salem/Walhalla, South Carolina, and is about three generations of women, about years of alienation and forgiveness. It is called

Three Parker Women, and I have another novel, not of the "Ladies" series, also to be published, called *A Change in the Landscape of Love,* which is a mature story with mother/daughter complications.

Do you work in other genres?

No, I love the novel—fiction form.

Talk about promoting your books.

I love meeting my readers. Promotion is hard whether you are with a big publisher, small one or you self-publish. It is hard work, lots of driving to bookstores often for one or two-three-five readers to show up. You get twenty-five people at an event, it's celebration time—until you make the big time, unless your pub or your readership make you a best seller. That's where the crowds are. Authors truly pay their dues.

Selected bibliography of Joan Medlicott

Fiction:

A Covington Christmas
The Spirit of Covington
The Gardens of Covington
A Home in Covington
From the Heart of Covington
The Ladies of Covington Send Their Love
The Three Mrs. Parkers

Barbara Robinette Moss

Barbara Robinette Moss announced her intention to be an artist in second grade. While the initial impulse may have been to get her mother's attention, the child's imagination and love for art has never left Moss. After completing a BFA from the Ringling School of Art and Design in Sarasota, Florida, and an MFA from Drake University in Des Moines, Iowa, Barbara Robinette Moss supported herself and her son working full-time as an artist. Along the way, writing "found her."

Her first memoir, *Change Me Into Zeus's Daughter*, garnered critical support, writing awards, and is being taught in several women's studies programs around the country. *Fierce*, her highly-anticipated second memoir, is available in hardcover. Moss had taken images from both books as "topics" for her artwork.

Barbara Robinette Moss modestly hopes her work touches people, and that by telling her story, she can help other women break the negative cycles in their own lives.

You've spent your entire adult life working as an artist. What impulse caused the change from visual arts to literary arts?

I've been making art all my life. I didn't choose writing over artwork. As I got older, the stories from my childhood came flooding back to me. I started writing on my artwork, bits of stories, but ultimately, the artwork wasn't big enough to hold my thoughts.

Writing came in search of me. Sometimes I'd get up in the middle of the night and write and write. I chose art as a career. Writing chose me. It's seems that the art and the writing are so connected, almost impossible to separate now.

Is *Fierce* a sequel to *Change Me into Zeus's Daughter?*

Both books hold up on their own. *Fierce* is not a sequel. I say that…yet, the second one picks up where the first one left off.

Describe your visual art.

It's very personal. The name of the upcoming show is titled: *Anything Personal.* There's one mixed-media piece featuring my mother's trunk. When we were kids, both our parents had trunks. They held our parents' military uniforms and records, ribbons, baby shoes, report cards. In the title piece, my mother's trunk is open with her personal items magically lifting into the air.

There's also a piece called *The Gypsy House.* In Eastaboga, just outside of Anniston [Alabama, the author's hometown], there's a tiny pink house. When I was a little girl, a family lived there. They would disappear and come back. The neighborhood called them gypsies—I think they were from Romania. The house was like a dollhouse, and inside there were a number of bird cages with different kinds of birds in each. I thought that house held a special kind of magic. The last time I was home, I made sketches of it. It's just about to fall to the ground, and I wanted to capture some little part of it before it vanished.

You've lived outside of the South for many years now. Do you feel Midwestern?

Gosh, no. I'm Southern to the bone. I think, write, make art as a Southerner.

Over the years, people have said, "You might want to consider getting rid of your Southern accent." But I won't—even if I could. This is me. This is who I am.

One of the central themes of *Fierce* is your devotion to your son and how hard you worked to give him everything you never had, particularly a stable childhood. What's he doing?

Jason is in chiropractic school in Kansas City. He's married to a lovely woman named Lindsey. He's a really good guy. He's avoided a lot of the pitfalls of being raised in poverty.

My dad was a major presence in *Zeus's Daughter* and Jason is a major presence in *Fierce*. As my son was getting older, I used him as a sounding board. He was aware that something in my life wasn't working...when your kid knows...well.

My intention from the day he was born was for him to have what I didn't have—all the kisses, all the love, all the attention, all the opportunities. In the larger picture, I was trying to give my son a fresh life—not one embedded in poverty or addiction.

The structure in *Fierce* is radically different from the structure in *Zeus's Daughter.*

In *Zeus's Daughter*, the narrative is more linear. *Fierce* is more like a quilt. I started with the stories that hurt the most. I thought that if I could live through writing those down, I would be all right, and could tell the rest of the story. I wanted to tell the truth.

Three or four chapters were very difficult to write. I didn't hold back. I thought, I can always take it out later. But I didn't take anything out. I hope someone will be able to use my experiences to help them in their own life.

I've heard that writing is like cutting open a vein. You have to get down to it. You tell the truth—no matter how difficult it is to face.

I was addicted. Not to alcohol, but still addicted. Sometimes people say, "I just don't GET it." I say, "Honey, you're just not old enough."

In *Fierce*, my addiction is paralleled with my brother's [alcoholism]. People tend to think addiction is only one thing. But women tend to choose other kinds of addictions. I was addicted to emotional pain—which I fed through bad relationships with men. I knew all about that, learned it as a girl, it was familiar.

To get better, to make my life work, I had to recognize what I was doing wrong. I was like a hamster on a wheel...I needed help. I found an amazing counselor—one who knew all the right things to say and do.

How does your family feel about the personal nature of your books?

Though sometimes what I write about family is hurtful to them, ultimately, I write for them. My parents are dead, and I still write for them too.

I try to see the bigger picture. Hopefully, what I write will live beyond anything I can imagine.

Have you started your third book?

I've recently moved to New York City where I'm studying playwrighting at the Actors Studio Drama School. I'm attempting to write a play. I love it—and it's so scary.

I'm also working on another book. The working title is *Lucky Girl*. It's about my mother and grandmother. Mostly, it's about my relationship with my mother.

What I do doesn't feel like work. Writing and making art transcends this universe. Breathing it is fresh—joyous—something indescribable.

When I was younger, I worked for my dad at a company that made screws and metal pieces. My job was to examine tiny screws as they came off the conveyor belt and throw them in a bucket of oil. As I worked, my mind would slip away to art making. I didn't realize I was working on stories. They were very much in my mind like plays. I'd love to write a play or screenplay for *Zeus's Daughter* or *Fierce*. That's how I wound up in New York City. I guess we'll see what happens next.

Do you have any particular writing process?

When I'm writing a book, I write 500 words a day on workdays. On weekends, I read them over to stay connected to the dream. Some days, when I find out I've written 1600 words, I'm happy out of my mind!

I taught myself to write by transposing my favorite books onto my computer.

I typed James Baldwin's *Go Tell it on the Mountain,* Toni Morrison's *Jazz,* Dorothy Allison's *Bastard Out of Carolina,* Harper Lee's *To Kill a Mockingbird,* Claude Brown's *Manchild in the Promised Land,* Faulkner's short stories "Spotted Ponies," and "The Bear," and all of Stephen Crane's poetry.

They all knew what they were doing and I thought transposing their work onto the computer would help the process sink into my head. I'm not totally self-taught. At Drake, Sharon Oard Warner read my first short story to the entire class, which meant so much to me. She was very encouraging. Mary Swander was also very influential; helped me with plot.

Are there any writers you recommend who may be of the literary mainstream?

James A. Autry. He's a jewel. Writes beautifully. I love *Nights Under a Tin Roof,* and *Life After Mississippi.* If you haven't read them, you must.

While I was writing *Fierce,* I got stuck; couldn't find my way out of the dark. I sent the manuscript to Jim. He read it, and immediately knew how to fix the problem. I'm not sure that manuscript would have made it to publication without his help. He was very generous with his time. He's also working on a new book. I can't wait to read it.

Selected bibliography of Barbara Robinette Moss

Fiction:

Change Me Into Zeus's Daughter
Fierce

Ron Rash

Ron Rash has a strong sense of place. His grandfather's "magical" stories and his family's Appalachian heritage form the basis for much of his work. Starting with "one image," his novels are about the dying of a culture, love of—and for—the land, and the influence of the dead on the living. *Saints at the River*, Rash's most recent work, was chosen for the seventh Southeastern Bookseller's Award in Fiction and the 2004 Southern Book Critics Award.

Where are you from?

My family has lived in the Appalachian Mountains since the mid-1700s—both families, my mother's and my father's are from here—which is why I focus on the South Appalachians as a setting. I grew up in Boiling Springs, North Carolina. It's between Charlotte and Asheville. It's also the home of Earl Scruggs.

Where did you go to college?

I attended Gardner-Webb in North Carolina and Clemson. I have a BA and a MA in English. I have found the intense reading I did at Clemson of great benefit.

Your first works weren't novels...

My first published work was a collection of stories [*The Night Jesus Fell to Earth*]. Then I worked in poetry for almost a decade. I didn't consciously set out to write novels. Both started with a single image I first tried to make into a poem.

After publishing three collections of poetry, earning an NEA poetry fellowship, and publishing two collections of short stories, you're "an overnight success" as a novelist...Discuss your transition in genres.

I'm a narrative poet, which makes the transition to fiction easier. As far as being "an overnight success," I've spent the last twenty-six years of my life writing seriously. I averaged three to five hours a day six days a week. I'm fifty now, and I've worked for a long time. I'm glad what success I've had has come slowly, because it has allowed me to work under the radar and concentrate solely on my writing. I've also had the example of writers such as Fred Chappell and Robert Morgan who both write poetry and fiction.

What do your two novels—*One Foot in Eden* and *Saints at the River*—have in common?

Both books are set in the same landscape, the same county, Oconee, in the most mountainous corner of South Carolina, located along the North Carolina border. Some of the same obsessions as well, especially the impact of the dead on the living, the erasure of a culture, the way landscape affects people psychologically.

Earlier you mentioned that there was always "one image" in your head starting each of your works. What was the "one image" for *Saints at the River?*

The first image was of a child's face looking up through water.

I wanted to write a novel about environmental issues, but one that refused simplifications. I picked a situation where I was essentially in conflict with myself, the part of me who is an environmentalist and the part of me who is a parent.

What was the "one image" in *One Foot in Eden?*

A farmer standing in his field, crops dying around him. He had a look of desperation of his face that transcended the drought.

What do you enjoy most about book signings and readings?

One thing is meeting people who've heard or read my work and found something there that has given them pleasure. I've also enjoyed meeting other writers. Particularly in the South, there's a real sense of camaraderie among writers.

What's your most amusing "author event" story?

My first public reading EVER was at the New York Public Library. I was thirty-two and had won the General Electric Younger Writers Award. I asked them to mail me the prize money but they said I had to come to New York and do the reading to get the money. I really needed the money so I went. I told myself I'd never see any of those people again and, besides, they'd never understand my accent. It turned out to be a wonderful experience.

Does book promotion interfere with writing?

I worry about the danger of getting away from writing. I travel with a laptop and try to work two to three hours every morning because I don't want to get out of the rhythm of writing.

What's your next book?

A novel, set in western North Carolina. It's set for a winter '06 publication with Holt.

You hold the John Parris Chair in Appalachian Studies at Western Carolina University. How do you balance writing, teaching, book events, and family life?

I have no real social life, except the book-promotion events. I rarely go to parties. I don't belong to the Moose Club or go out to bars. I'd rather spend time at home with my family.

What advice do you give your students regarding writing?

Read as much as possible and read widely. Persevere. Too many good writers give up too quickly. Perseverance is underrated in creative writing. For most of us, who are not Shakespeare or Keats, it takes work.

Whose works do you include in your Appalachian Literature courses?

Lee Smith, Robert Morgan, Fred Chappell, Silas House, Pam Duncan, James Still, Harriet Arnow, Jeff Daniel Marion, and many more fine writers.

Who are some of the writers readers should be reading or who should be better known?

I believe the greatest living American writer is Cormac McCarthy. No one writing today can match his level of language, especially in *Blood Meridian.*

As far as being underrated, Donald Harington from the Ozark Mountain region. His work is tremendously underrated; Chris Holbrook out of Kentucky; and Catherine Landis. I think she's the real deal.

Have you had mentors?

Lee Smith and Robert Morgan have been supportive and their work important to me. They are both exceptional writers and exceptional human beings.

What have you been waiting for someone to ask?

"What is it that makes someone become a writer?" I have vivid memories of my grandfather—who couldn't read or write. I asked him to read *Cat in the Hat* and he made up a story. He always "read" it differently. His stories were more entertaining than my mother's. He taught me language can be magical.

Selected bibliography of Ron Rash

Fiction:

The Night Jesus Fell to Earth and Other Stories from Cliffside, North Carolina
One Foot in Eden
Saints at the River

Poetry:

Among the Believers
Casualties
Eureka Mill
Raising the Dead

Jeanne Ray

At the 2003 "Southern Voices: Cross Roads & Common Threads" conference at the Hoover Public Library (Alabama), Jeanne Ray described becoming "the unwitting poster woman for change" in the last five years. Calling change "big and ambitious," she told the audience, "Until three years ago, when I started doing publicity for my books, the closest I came to public speaking was ordering at the drive-up line at Wendy's."

When Ray, who graduated from nursing school in 1958, started writing, the first question she asked herself was, "What do my heroines do for a living?" Describing her childhood with Depression-era parents as "both a cliché and understatement," Ray gave her parents credit for her work ethic. "If my parents had told me the 'Cinderella' story, Cinderella would have skipped the ball to take a typing test because she knew families always need two incomes."

After the publication of *Julie and Romeo* and *Step*Ball*Change*, Ray found herself "writing like a maniac" on the novel that became *Eat Cake*. Joking that she wanted "to publish as many books as possible before editors discovered she's a nurse with a computer," Ray acknowledged that writers have themes and the "job hang up" in each of her novels is the "literary equivalent of Charles Dickens' orphans."

Even though her books have been bestsellers, she laughs, saying, "In my dreams, I'm still a nurse. It sometimes takes a long time for the little pieces of ourselves to catch up with us."

Do you still work as a nurse? How do your dual careers play against one another?

I do still work as a nurse one day a week. I enjoy the relationships I have built up over the years, and value the grounding effect nursing has always had on me. I think my dual careers work hand in hand. I learn about life largely through my nursing and the writing allows me to record what I've learned.

How did you get into writing?

I have always written, but never with the intent of selling anything. I began *Julie and Romeo* because I thought someone should write a love story for people over sixty. When I had written about 150 pages, I showed it to my daughter, Ann [Patchett], who has a traditional writer's education. She liked what I had done and encouraged me to finish it. She also gave me editorial advice. Then when I had finished, Ann asked her own agent if she'd read the piece. It might have been easier to go for the MFA and skip having a talented daughter, but I wouldn't have it any other way!

What it's like having two writers in the family?

We love being able to "talk shop." It's wonderful, I think, for both of us.

You write about women "of a certain age" whose lives are in transition. Did you set out to write about the so-called "sandwich generation?"

I definitely chose to write about "sandwich generation" situations. Youth is wonderful, but we have a certain media overload. This "certain age" is a good time to be alive, vital, healthy, creative. And to remember to meet some of our own needs as well as those of others.

You've written three novels—all sequel-worthy. Is there any chance readers will see these families again?

I usually am a little tired of these people once I finish a book. But let's just say I still wonder how *Julie and Romeo* are doing every now and then.

One of the more interesting themes in American Literature is the ways people become families. Do you have any comments on the new American family?

I can only say that I agree entirely with you. Families, in all their many permutations, are fascinating. In nursing as well as in literature…I just think family problems are peculiar and funny and rewarding enough even when you're trying not to embroider them too much.

How much research did you put into the books? The first one has florists, the second tap dancing, and the most recent, baking.

I know a family (as a nurse) who own and run a florist shop. They let me "hang out" and ask questions. I have a friend who was a tap dancer and I asked a lot of questions. I don't dance, but LOVE to watch. I do bake. I learned to bake with my mother, and baked with my daughters. I adore the scent of something wonderful in the oven. I love giving baked goods away.

Did you have any literary mentors? Heroes or heroines?

Ann has certainly been my literary mentor. I have always read often and almost anything. Raymond Chandler taught me, as did Graham Greene and Evelyn Waugh. Gabriel Garcia Marquez taught me. Shakespeare taught me.

Is there any question you've been dying for someone to ask that you'd like to answer here?

Yes! "What is it that thrills you most about your new career?"

It gives me the opportunity to demonstrate to others the importance of embracing change, trying something new, digging deep into themselves and looking for a talent they'd enjoy sharing. It allows me to give people hope about themselves by telling them what happened to me.

Selected bibliography of Jeanne Ray

Fiction:

Julie and Romeo
Step*Ball*Change
Eat Cake
Julie and Romeo Get Lucky

Michelle Richmond

Michelle Richmond may well epitomize the contemporary Southerner. She's traveled the world, yet returns to the South of her childhood in her fiction—creating, expanding, and transcending what it means to be a Southern writer. Her first collection of short stories, *The Girl in the Fall-Away Dress,* won the Associated Writing Program's 2000 Award for Short Fiction, and her first novel, *Dream of the Blue Room,* was published by MacAdam/Cage. A second novel, *Ocean Beach,* is forthcoming from Bantam in the summer of 2006. Richmond's fictional women are running toward their futures rather than away from their pasts. After reading her work, it's hard to imagine she's not doing the same.

In what ways did your childhood influence your writing?

I grew up in Mobile, Alabama, the middle child among three daughters. Growing up with sisters had a profound impact on my writing, as did religion. My upbringing was of the fire-and-brimstone Southern Baptist sort, with Sunday school, "big church," and training union on Sundays, as well as Girls in Action and prayer meeting on Wednesday. From kindergarten through fifth grade, I went to an extremely strict parochial school where the girls were required to wear uniforms and the boys were not. During these years I think I formed an odd sense of humor, a morbid fascination with and appreciation for everyday absurdities, as well as some sense of the injustices that are so often perpetrated in the name of religion.

Even though I left Alabama ten years ago, the South is always with me, and the landscape and climate of my childhood is always a presence in my fiction. With *Dream of the Blue Room,* for example, I set out to write a novel about China; as it turned out, large portions of the novel are set in a small river town in Alabama. The protagonist of *Ocean Beach* lives in San Francisco but ruminates extensively about her childhood on the Gulf Coast.

When I was growing up, I always wanted to get away, to see something new, to seek out adventure in some unfamiliar part of the country. I've spent the bulk of my post-college years in New York City and San Francisco, but I am always acutely aware of an internal push-pull between the urban landscape I've chosen as an adult and the milder Gulf Coast/suburban landscape of my childhood.

What's your educational background?

I studied English and Journalism at the University of Alabama, then worked for three years as a magazine writer and advertising copywriter in Knoxville and Atlanta before going on to begin my MFA at the University of Arkansas and complete it at the University of Miami.

How have your MFA and various prizes benefited your writing?

I did my MFA at the University of Miami, one of many writing programs that was generously funded by James Michener. Being a Michener Fellow was beneficial in that it paid tuition and a good stipend, while requiring that I teach only one class per semester—a creative writing class—in addition to my graduate course load. This gave me ample time to write. It didn't hurt, of course, that I was living in a studio on the beach with an amazing view of the ocean. It was the ultimate "room of one's own," and I did more writing there than any time before or since.

I also spend a month each summer at a writers' colony. The Millay Colony for the Arts, the Saltonstall Foundation, Hedgebrook, and the Julia and David White Artists' Colony in Costa Rica have all been so generous as to offer me fully funded one-month residencies, including room and board. This is where I do the bulk of my writing. Since I teach full-time (and for several years I taught six or seven classes per semester, substantially more than a full-time load), it has often been a struggle to find time to write. When I go to a colony, everything I've been wanting to write for the past year comes flooding out. I haven't been able to find that level of privacy, and that kind of freedom to write, anywhere else.

The prize that has had the most significant impact on my career would have to be the Associated Writing Programs Award for Short Fiction, which I received in 2000 for my story collection, *The Girl in the Fall-Away Dress*. The winning manuscript each year is published by University of Massachusetts Press. This award allowed me to cross that elusive "first book" hurdle. It also allowed me to leave my job teaching heavily-enrolled composition courses for a much more comfortable position teaching in an MFA program. I have to plug the AWP here, because it provides a much-needed venue, along with awards like the Bakeless Prize and the Sandstone Prize, for non-commercial literary fiction by unknown writers. My semester-long stint as Distinguished Visiting Writer at Bowling Green State University allowed me to finish my latest novel, *Ocean Beach*.

Are there any particular writers who've influenced your work?

Walker Percy, whose novel *The Moviegoer* I read once a year; I think it's one of the most sad, beautiful books ever written. Jayne Anne Phillips, whose story collection *Black Tickets* was given to me in Arkansas by my professor, James Whitehead. Joy Williams, whose novel *State of Grace* I discovered in a sale bin in Knoxville when I was twenty-two. The Albanian writers Ismael Kadare, Jiri Kajane, the British writer Ian McEwan, and the German writer Heinrich Boll, four authors whose work I was introduced to by my husband. Borges, Calvino, and Nabokov. Chekhov, who ends his short story "Lady with a Pet Dog" with the shatteringly tragic and truthful line, "and it was clear to both of them that the end was still far off, and that what was to be most complicated and difficult for them was only just beginning."

Have all of these writers influenced me? I'm not sure. I just know that I pick up their books and think, "Wow, I wish I could do that." I read them again and again. And I can't discount the influence of the Bible, which I read and memorized passages of during my childhood and early adolescence; surely the language of the Bible, and those walloping passionate stories, embedded themselves somewhere in my head.

What do you write besides fiction?

Because I travel whenever I get the chance, I do some travel writing. I've written essays on China, Hungary, Iceland, Scotland, Argentina, and a number of other places. I also write the occasional personal essay. But fiction is really my first love. To me, fiction presents less of a structural challenge, because you're building the story from the ground up, rather than trying to "remodel" the truth and give it an aesthetically pleasing and sensible shape, which is what non-fiction requires.

Between the short story and the novel, I don't really have a preference, although each offers a different sort of challenge and reward. It's like the difference between hiking four miles along the Northern California Coast and climbing Mount Kilimanjaro: The hike on the beach is fun; it's not too strenuous and you're always in sight of your destination. When you get there, you feel pretty good, and you still have enough strength to call up some friends and go out for Chinese food in the evening.

And then there's Kilimanjaro. Halfway up the mountain you're out of breath and out of shape and wishing you'd never started; you're thinking you didn't pack the right equipment; you really want a martini; you want to climb back down, but you've made it this far, and you go on simply because you know you'll end up hating yourself if you don't. When you finally get to the top, you feel beaten up and worn out, but you also know you've accomplished something. You decide that you will never, ever climb Mount Kilimanjaro again; but inevitably there will be a moment of insanity, a moment when you think you're up to the task this time, and you'll start the whole process all over again.

How difficult was it for you to move from writing short stories into working on the novel? How long did it take to complete the novel?

When I was in graduate school, and for a year after grad school when I was living in New York City, I wrote a novel. It was a truly terrible novel. The novel was pretty funny, but unintentionally so; it was the novel's overwhelming and unabashed badness that, in hindsight, is amusing. Fortunately, during that period I was also writing short stories and was able to put together what would become my first book, *The Girl in the Fall-Away Dress*.

After the prolonged misery of that first failed novel, I was a little wary of starting a new one, but my husband Kevin badgered me until I did, and then he held my hand every step of the way. I wrote the novel during one-month spurts during three consecutive summers, between academic semesters. During the school year, while I was teaching full-time, I grabbed a few hours whenever I could to rewrite and restructure. When I was away writing, I would email Kevin my new pages every day, and he would email back his suggestions. When I got stuck and didn't know where to go, he would say, "Okay, now it's time to write this scene," and he would tell me what the scene needed to do, why it mattered. There were many times during the writing of *Dream of the Blue Room* that I seriously considered trashing the whole thing and starting over with a new idea. Ultimately, what kept me going was the same thing that keeps so many failing marriages going, the same thing that makes people stay in bad jobs—I'd invested too much time and energy, and I was determined not to let that go to waste.

The World's Most Rotten Novel, which is how I affectionately refer to my first grad school effort at the long fiction form, was actually a good experience.

It taught me a lot about what I should NOT do in my second novel. I learned so much from *Dream of the Blue Room* that writing *Ocean Beach* was somewhat easier—although it's never a sure formula. Each time you write a story or novel, you must, in some way, learn to crawl again.

How would you describe your publishing experiences?

Publishing? Well, that's hell. It's the most difficult thing, in my opinion, that a writer has to do. Just getting someone to care about what you've written, to believe in it, is as frustrating and discouraging as trying to tear the thin plastic backing off of contact paper.

After my story collection came out, an acquisitions editor for a large publishing house asked to see my novel. I got all excited and sent the manuscript, only to receive a letter a few weeks later in which she explained that, although she liked the writing and the story was engaging, my novel had two major problems—and I quote, "There's a sense that there's just too much Chinese-ness out there in the market today. Also, lesbian themes don't sell well. That's two big strikes against the novel." She went on to say that, if I would "consider changing these elements," she'd be happy to read the novel again. So there I was with a novel set mainly in China, fueled largely by the narrator's adolescent love affair with another girl, and this woman convinced me that no publisher would ever touch it.

Several months later, enter Frank Turner Hollon, author of *The God File* and *Pains of April*. I'd never met Frank, but in the summer of 2002 he happened to be doing a signing at a bookstore in Alabama. It was a slow day in the store, so he picked up a book to read between customers; it was *The Girl in the Fall-Away Dress*. A couple of days later he called Sonny Brewer, who does a lot to promote Southern writers through his wonderful bookstore in Fairhope, Alabama, Over the Transom.

Sonny had brought Frank to the attention of the San Francisco publisher MacAdam/Cage a couple of years before, and had since developed a strong relationship with

MacAdam/Cage. After reading *The Girl in the Fall-Away Dress*, Sonny contacted me and asked if I had a novel. I did.

The publication of *Ocean Beach* came about in a more traditional way. I met a wonderful agent, Anne Borchardt, at the Sewanee Writers' Conference and she offered to represent my book. Valerie Borchardt then tirelessly sent the book out and eventually sold it to Bantam.

I've found that Alabama embraces its writers warmly, even those of us who have left home, so it felt very natural for me to come into the publication of this book by way of a cross-pollination between Alabama, where I spent the first twenty-two years of my life, and San Francisco, my adopted home.

Would you like to talk about your family?

I got married a couple of years ago to a wonderful guy named Kevin whom I met in grad school. He's also a writer, and he's very much in tune with my writing. Much of what I write I see as a collaboration. He helped me to formulate the plot for *Dream of the Blue Room*, and he read the manuscript in its various manifestations dozens of times, offering suggestions on how to strengthen characters, add depth to the story, etc.

For *Ocean Beach*, he and I came up with the idea for the novel, the nugget of the story, together.

We're also collaborating now on a longer-term project, Oscar, who was born in December 2004, and is not very amenable to his mother's passionate pursuit of a writing career.

I have a sister in Birmingham, and my mother lives in Mobile. My dad is in Memphis and my younger sister lives in San Francisco. My extended family is in Mississippi.

I return to the South frequently. What I miss most about the South are warm summer nights—sitting on a screened-in porch or eating seafood out on a pier, with a very, very cold beer.

How did growing up in a female-dominated household influence your work?

I was blessed to grow up with two sisters; one is a year and a half older than I, and the other is eight years younger. Thus I had the great advantage of being a little sister for eight years before taking on the role of protective big sister. In *The Girl in the Fall-Away Dress*, sisterhood is a recurring theme, and is structurally the link that holds all the stories together.

The major characters in almost all of my stories, as well as in my novel, are women—flawed but hopefully resilient women who are ultimately responsible for their own downfall or deliverance. In many of my earlier stories, such as "The Last Bad Thing," the narrative is intentionally structured to reflect the fragmentary nature of modern life, particularly for women. This is also true in the title story of "The Girl in the Fall-Away Dress," in which a woman from Alabama finally finds her home and her independence in San Francisco, meanwhile discovering parallels with the life her mother lived thirty years before. *Dream of the Blue Room* is, in large part, about the intimate relationships among young girls that in so many ways shape our later years and adult relationships.

What is your next project?

I'm currently two hundred pages into a new novel. This one is set on the beach a couple of miles down from my house. However, the narrator is from Alabama and scenes from her Alabama childhood have a definite presence in the novel.

Where do you teach?

I teach in the MFA Program in Writing at the University of San Francisco and California College of the Arts. I love teaching, particularly the undergraduates. How many jobs allow one to foist one's own literary tastes upon a helpless and captive audience? You're sitting in a room with fifteen or so students crowded around a table, and you're doing your spiel about such and such novel, such and such writer, and you're asking questions, and the students are responding, and maybe a couple of them are doodling in the margins of their course readers, but at least a couple of them are looking at you with this rapt expression, as if what you're telling them is something they want to know, as if they really get it. I've never gotten that kind of rush from an office job.

While your work has some deeply Southern components (the Baptist Church, the Pentecostals, etc.), it also transcends any regional labeling...

I've moved around a lot, and I've done a great deal of traveling. Places stick in my mind—the natural and manmade architecture of a place, the character of its people, the climate.

These things find their way into my writing without any real intent on my part. *The Girl in the Fall-Away Dress* contains stories set in Mobile, Atlanta, Knoxville, New York City, San Francisco, and Arkansas—all places where I have lived.

The emotional heart of *Dream of the Blue Room* is in a small river town in Alabama. My identity was formed on the Gulf Coast, the bulk of my memory is grounded there, but as time passes these other places where I've made my bed have also taken root in my mind and have become fertile ground for fiction.

Do you label yourself in any way?

Well, I suppose I might be classified as a "Southern writer," in that I grew up in the South and much of my work is set in the South and very much defined by place. I do have a profound respect for the literature that has come our of the South; however, I shy away from this categorization simply because I think my literary development may owe more to Eastern European and non-Southern American writers than it does to Southern icons like Eudora Welty or Flannery O'Connor.

Where do you see yourself in ten years? Twenty years?

Hopefully, both the work and I will be leaner, stronger, wiser, and more mature in ten to twenty years.

Selected bibliography Michelle Richmond

Fiction:

The Girl in the Fall-Away Dress
Dream of the Blue Room
Ocean Beach

Jeff Sharlet

The Bible contains many of humanity's most enduring stories. In the reading of the first few chapters of Genesis alone, readers learn that life isn't always fair, people aren't always kind, and families can be particularly cruel to one another. It might even be safe to argue these stories have become a part of the Western collective unconscious.

Peter Manseau and Jeff Sharlet, founding editors of the online magazine *Killing the Buddha,* approached thirteen contemporary authors, asking each to retell a story from the Bible. In the introduction, the editors write "Like everyone else who knows how to read or count the stars, we've spent our whole lives studying scripture." Manseau and Sharlet set out to talk with Americans about belief. On their yearlong road trip, they drove south, west, then north and back, discovering the width and breadth of religious belief in this country. The resulting collection, *Killing the Buddha: A Heretic's Bible,* is one of the best reads of the year.

On page three of *Killing the Buddha,* you wrote, "Because all the people we spoke to told us it was no coincidence we showed up." Do you believe, as Bill Moyers says, "Coincidence is God's way of remaining anonymous?"

Hmm. That's a good question. It's tempting to say yes, because it's a good metaphor, but no. Sometimes a cigar is just a cigar. Which when you think about it is even more thrilling. Here's this staggeringly complex system, a machine so grand and intricate that it is truly random, and two parts that will click—writers and people with great stories—sweep past each other unpredictably. I'd like to think God is as delighted by the surprise as we are.

Would you like to introduce yourself and your co-editor?

Peter Manseau and I met in the late '90s, working at a strange, brilliant little nonprofit called the National Yiddish Book Center. Yiddish was the secular language of Eastern European Jews. With a few exceptions, it's extinct now. So our job was to find and preserve the books that had been written in this language. People threw them away, since they didn't know what they were. We hauled them out of the trash. So that gave Peter and me a model for thinking about stories. You need to go out and save the ones others would just throw away. After we left that organization, me for journalism, Peter for academe, we stayed in touch through *KillingTheBuddha.com*. When we were invited to make a book of it, we at first thought we'd just write some essays. Then we had the idea of a kind of dinner party, with all kinds of other writers. Our own writing in conversation with theirs.

How were the contributing writers for the book selected?

Primarily as the result of a lifetime of passionate reading, followed by a binge of reading to acquaint ourselves with anyone we hadn't heard of. We weren't looking for big names, or authorities, or even the finest writers, although we ended up with a few of each. We were interested in people who dealt with religion "implicitly." There are writers whom we love, like Kathleen Norris or James Carroll, who are dead-on in their approach to religion. But for this, we were more interested in the sideways approach. And then there was coincidence. We were in South Carolina when I got a phone call from le thi diem thuy, who wrote our "Book of Ruth." She'd read an essay of mine, about the death of my mother, and wanted to talk about it. Her own mother had just died, and she'd taken her to back to

Vietnam for the funeral. As it happened, Peter and I were spending a lot of time with a young mother, herself the daughter of members of a sort of benign cult, and we were thinking a lot about mothers and daughters and the book of Ruth when le thi diem thuy called. I'll grant that one was maybe divine providence.

What was the co-editing process like for you? The two of you?

A battle, trench warfare every step of the way. And we're glad it was. There are some popular myths about writing, authorship, and collaboration. The idea that writing comes from an ethereal muse, or that a single author conceives a story (never happened; it's always a collaboration of some kind), and that the best collaborations are a meeting of like minds. Uh-uh. What makes *Killing the Buddha* work is that we disagreed on "a lot," and so we had to talk, often pretty passionately, about what it should be. The result is so much better and smarter than what either of us on our own could have accomplished. We think that might be a model for religious community, too. It's not about finding people who believe just like you do. It's about being in a church, or a temple, or gathered around a campfire singing, and you need to sing along with people whose voices ain't always pretty. You need to work with the guy you think has it all wrong. You need to recognize that his or her god is as real, in some senses, as your is. That's collaboration. Anything else is an echo chamber.

Is there any simple answer to the question, "What did you learn while putting together the book?"

Compassion. Not sympathy, but compassion, an appreciation for the suffering and joy of everyone you meet. Suffering and joy are intrinsic to most religious or spiritual belief, in a way that they're not involved in any other aspect of our lives. You want to see all God's creation? Then you need to learn to look with compassionate eyes. It's hard. We often failed. But we learned through doing the book that it's not something you can give up on. Compassion is a work in progress.

Were any of the trip's highlights cut out of the book? What didn't make the final cut?

Oh, lordy! All told, we traveled for about a year, spread out over two years. The stories we didn't tell! In Miami, we got cursed by a Santeria shop owner (Santeria is a combination of West African religions and Catholicism, popular with Cubans) who thought we were spies from Castro. Some spies—neither of us even speaks Spanish. She sprayed a "magic" oil on us. Twenty minutes later, we both got splitting headaches. Sometimes we brought this kind of trouble on ourselves. In Chimayo, New Mexico, we both ate dirt, along with several thousand Catholic pilgrims who believe it has healing power there. Not bad. Kind of gritty. But bad for the stomach, it turns out. In Crestone, Colorado, we spent a week living about a labyrinth. In Troy, Alabama, we had a great time in a bar with a couple of sorority girls and an old homeless drifter. Sounds seedy, I know, but it wasn't—we all just got into telling and hearing stories about religion, each of us coming from a totally different world. And getting fall-down drunk but never losing hold of the storytelling. It really was a religious service.

What was your most memorable day of writing?

I think for me it was drafting [the chapter of] the skeleton of Broward County, Florida. Usually one of us would just start writing about something, and the other guy would then jump in and join the riffing. The Broward County chapter is about this really dark spell we'd gone through in Miami, where we'd gone to look for Santeria. The Cuban Americans wouldn't talk to us— they thought we were spies. One of our computers got stolen. And we wound up attending this church of fascist (literally) Caribbean exiles. One of their own had been murdered by a false preacher who turned out to be a serial killer. He'd been convicted, and they had the most rousing gospel service I've attended, to celebrate—and to pray that he get the electric chair. They sang "Power in the Blood" with a whole new meaning. So I started writing this up a week later, recovering sort of, at a friend's house in Nashville. We'd met up a great songwriter there, Clare Burson, and I sat in my friend's living room listening to one of Clare's CDs—one song in particular, "Mysteries Revealed"—over and over even as I hummed "Power in the Blood" to myself and wrote the skeleton of that chapter, which is essentially just a long, long song about this vengeance gospel choir, about race, blood, lies...It was a terrifying experience. Now, if I listen to a beautiful rendition of "Power in the Blood" like Mahalia Jackson's, it still scares me. I remember sitting there and thinking, realizing deep in my bones: Faith is dangerous. It can be.

You've been touring, promoting the book, what question have you not been asked that you'd still like to be asked or were hoping you'd be asked?

"Can we buy movie rights?" Actually, some guy did ask us that, but he was crazy. No movie deal yet. Otherwise, readers are really pretty smart. They asked good, tough questions, more than I could have imagined. I was surprised that not many picked up on—or asked about, anyway—the political subtext of the book. It's very much about democracy, a radical idea of democracy. It's a dark book in a lot of ways, but I think that's where the hope in it lies—the discovery that there is this incredible, raw, democratic impulse in even the most authoritarian—or the most flaky—faiths. Everyone wanted to convert us, but when they didn't, they wanted the conversation to continue. People love free speech. They love storytelling. And that, to me, is democracy.

What would you say specifically about the South as a locale in your travels?

The South is well-represented. Darcey Steinke, Haven Kimmel, Randall Kenan, April Reynolds. New York City is probably better represented, but that's not surprising given the economic realities of publishing in America (aside: The South needs more publishing houses!) The Southern stories we told: a Pentecostal exorcism in Henderson, North Carolina; a Baba lover compound in Myrtle Beach, South Carolina; Broward County,

Florida; an itinerant preacher from Alabama, who we ran into in central Florida; Nashville, which was just this swirl of things, a church that had been turned into a brothel; the death of Waylon Jennings; a mosque that prayed to Jesus for protection from violent Christians...Mt. Vernon, Texas, where we went to a cowboy church...There'a a lot of South in there. One thing that made us sad was that our publisher—really first rate, by the way, and that's not flattery—nonetheless was just a little blind to the South. We traveled all over the country on the book tour, but except for a great week in North Carolina, skipped the South. But that's not just our publisher's fault. That's the reality of book buying in the South. The South needs more bookstores. More publishing houses. It needs to look to its literary future as well as its glorious past. No more faux Faulkners! (and I LOVE Faulkner). More attention to what's happening now. *Southern Scribe, Oxford American,* these things are great. But the South needs more. And the rest of the country needs that to come from the South, too.

Are you likely to write a sequel?

We're making a radio documentary about the people we met on the book tour that should play on NPR's "All Things Considered" this fall. And we both sold second books—Peter's is called *Vows,* about his family—his father is a Catholic priest, his mother is a former nun. I'm working on one called *Power in the Blood,* which is an exploration of the dangerous side of faith.

Talk about your website.

KillingTheBuddha.com is sort of like the ongoing experience of the book. It's an unpredictable congregation. Reportage, memoirs, even recipes—anything that reveals the presence of religion in the world and the world in religion. Lately, I've been putting a lot of energy into a new website as well, *The Revealer* (www.therevealer.org), a daily review of religion and the press—looking at the way stories about religion get told.

Selected bibliography Jeff Sharlet

Non-fiction:

Killing the Buddha: A Heretic's Bible (co-editor along with Peter Manseau)

Kay Sloan

Warmth emanates from Kay Sloan. Her conversation is filled with concern for her family, her students, and the world at large.

The Mississippi of her childhood holds a prominent place in her fiction as do the voices she heard growing up there. Her first novel, *Worry Beads*, won the Ohioana Award for Fiction, and her second novel, *The Patron Saint of the Red Chevys*, has won two nominations in "young adult fiction."

In addition to her short stories, essays, and poetry, Dr. Sloan has published a book on American cultural studies and a book on silent films. She teaches English and American Studies at Miami University of Ohio.

Introduce yourself.

I was born in Hattiesburg, Mississippi—my father, who worked for the telephone company, was transferred to the Gulf Coast. We lived in Biloxi until I was five years old, and those years are imprinted in my memory: the free-wheeling nightlife and easy laughter of adults, the childhood fun of the beach and Ship Island. We then moved to Jackson, and later I attended Millsaps College for a couple of years. I then left for California at age twenty, and graduated from the University of California at Santa Cruz with a degree in sociology. My MA and PhD in American Studies are from the University of Texas at Austin. I now teach at Miami University of Ohio—the vagaries of the academic job market drew me to the Midwest. I met my husband, David Schloss, a poet, at Miami University; we have a ten year-old daughter who is also a writer.

You mentioned that your daughter gave you the opening line of *The Patron Saint of the Red Chevys*, did she give you the opening line? The first image? Both?

When my daughter was four, she was very unhappy with me about the fact that she had to eat some green vegetables before she could have ice cream. Her response was a sullen "I'm gonna kill you." The dialogue between mother and daughter continued on a civil basis—a back and forth about learning to be independent—until she was feeling cuddly with me rather than so mischievous. I realized later that she'd given me some interesting dialogue!

How long have you been writing?

Like my daughter, I wrote when I was a child. During the summer breaks from elementary school, I'd write what I called "novels" with a pencil on lined paper. As an adult, I've felt as if my writing self were divided between the creative side of poetry, fiction, and essays, and then the scholarly side of historical writing. My first publication was a poem, "The First Glaciers," written to my mother, published in *Southern Exposures*, in my twenties.

My first book grew from a paper I wrote in graduate school on the Edward Harriman Expedition to Alaska in 1899. It has to be the most bizarre exploring expedition in history. Harriman was a railroad "robber baron," and when his doctor ordered rest after he bought the Union Pacific Railroad, Harriman decided to organize an exploring expedition to Alaska as his "restful" vacation. So he signed on the nation's top scientists and writers—even John Muir was on board. Later, the piece grew into a full length book, *Looking Far North: The Harriman Expedition to Alaska, 1899,* which I co-authored with one of my professors, a very talented writer and historian, William H. Goetzmann, who had won the Pulitzer Prize for an earlier book. At any rate, the fun thing about this book was that for many years, I always thought that someday, someone would re-create that expedition. Sure enough, about three years ago, I got a phone call from a PBS filmmaker who was making a documentary about the expedition, and wanted me to go along on the re-creation of the voyage. It was wonderful fun to see the places and sites that my historical "characters" had visited over one hundred years before. The documentary, "The 1899 Harriman Alaska Expedition Retraced," was aired in the summer of 2003.

My other historical book is on silent movies—really early silent movies—from just after the turn of the century. I was interested in how the cinema—as a brand-new invention and art form—was defining itself. This book, *The Loud Silents*, looks at movies that made great protagonists from woman suffragists, corrupt politicians, and even prostitutes. Thinking that people needed to see these films as well as read about them, I made a documentary called "Suffragettes in the Silent Cinema."

Discuss your first work of fiction.

My first novel, *Worry Beads*, is about secrets of a Southern family that have been kept for decades, and how a hidden history comes out through old home movies that the younger family members are restoring for an upcoming family reunion. What is never discovered is a love affair that a World War II veteran named Fred had with his brother's wife, Virginia. It, too, is set in Mississippi, and scattered through time, from the 1940s to the 1980s. I had a wonderful time writing it.

What did you learn from writing/publishing *Worry Beads* that saved you time when you were writing *The Patron Saint of the Red Chevys?*

One thing that comes to mind is that, while writing *Worry Beads* with lots of a first-novelist's optimism and enthusiasm, I never doubted that it would find a publisher. Though it took longer than I expected, *Worry Beads* was published by Louisiana State University Press in 1991. When I was writing *The Patron Saint of Red Chevys*, I knew that no magic doors would open when

I finished it—but one writes from love for the characters in the work, anyway, not love of publication. In terms of technique, Eudora Welty has said that each novel has a different way of being told, a different path to follow. I'd have to say that *Worry Beads* may have been actually easier to write because I had more enthusiasm about the publishing world. Also, the style in which it was written, which is mostly present-tense vignettes from the home movies, was somewhat easier to approach than the more traditional, chronological narrative that I had in *The Patron Saint of Red Chevys*.

The Patron Saint of the Red Chevys been promoted as "young adult fiction." Was it your intention to write for the young adult market?

It surprised me that *The Patron Saint of Red Chevys* won two nominations for a "young adult" readership. I didn't have that market in mind, but it's nice to know that the American Library Association thought the "coming of age" aspect would be illuminating and educational for teenagers. I still envision the novel for adult readers, and I've had wonderful comments from them.

What's the best advice you were given as a young writer?

"Have no self-doubt." That's what a professor of mine, Archie Green, once told me in graduate school. I do think that publishing is a combination of talent, perseverance and luck, and not necessarily in that order. William Goetzmann was a terrific teacher of writing for me, too, as I saw that writing historical narrative could be filled with lively characters, action, dialogue, and lyrical description. And it was up to the author, not the subject matter necessarily, to provide that. I would tell an aspiring writer in this era of publishing to write what you're passionate about, and to write it without caring if it ever gets published. And—to have no self-doubt!

Does living in Ohio give you the necessary distance to write about your home?

When I was writing *Worry Beads*, I moved to the Gulf Coast to complete it, and added some of the best scenes, I think. So, in other words, I'm not sure that we really need physical distance from the cultures we write about in order to capture them. But emotional distance is a good thing. No doubt, the six years I spent in California helped me get a handle on the events and experiences that I wanted to write about. It's funny that I've never written fiction about Southern Ohio, though. Only a couple of poems. And place is very important to me. After about twenty years here, I still haven't figured out how Southern Ohio has become part of me.

Were you aware—as a child growing up in Mississippi—of the great tradition of writers in the state?

As a child, I used to see Eudora Welty in Jackson's downtown library, slowly walking down the aisles, perusing the shelves. So yes, I was quite aware of how rich a literary legacy Mississippi has, and I learned a lot from reading Southern writers when I was out living in the Santa Cruz Mountains. I immersed myself in Faulkner, Welty, O'Connor, McCullers, Williams…hoping to find a way to re-connect to the South, to my home. The literature helped a great deal. The writer is an outsider, I think, who lives on the boundary of the culture, like an outlaw, observing, watching, recording even while experiencing. Southern writers also seemed to validate the sense of alienation I often felt from the South in the 1960s. I can't say that the tradition of great Southern literature felt like a heavy burden, though, since I don't compare myself to those writers. If they were writing contemporaries of mine, then, yes, it probably would feel like a burden!

Is place or character more important in your work?

That's almost impossible to say, since when a character pops into my head, he or she is always connected to a place. They just seem inseparable. I usually start with characters, but place is attached to them. It defines who they are and how they think.

Presumably you were aware of the civil rights movement during your childhood. What are some of the changes you hope to see in this country within your lifetime?

Yes, the civil rights movement was a great presence in my childhood, forcing me to either accept or reject what the adult white culture told me. It was stressful and confusing as a child, trying to sort out the truth in a racist environment that included the church, the school, family friends—and my own school friends.

I think our country is still facing the challenge of giving civil rights to all of our citizens, regardless of their skin color, sexual preference, or country of birth. If terrorists can dictate that we start limiting civil rights, then they have already won a victory in eroding the democratic principles so fundamental to our way of life.

What's your idea of perfect happiness?

Perfect happiness! A few years ago, I might have said that it would be sitting in a café on Santorini or Corfu, in the brilliant Greek sun, sipping a glass of wine and watching the blue sea with my husband while our daughter played in the sand. (We did live in Greece when she was two, and it was wonderful.)

In today's world, though, I'll give a more serious answer. In a state of perfect happiness, one would feel safe and content in the culture in which one lives. Right now, we have such great divisions in America, the deepest that I've ever seen in my lifetime, and a terrible war in the Middle East that seems more likely to deepen those divisions than to secure our safety. We have had a society built on the idea of fostering "life, liberty, and the pursuit of happiness" for all, and I only hope that that beautiful goal can survive the crises that we will face in the upcoming years.

Selected bibliography of Kay Sloan

Fiction:

Worry Beads
The Patron Saint of Red Chevys

Non-fiction:

The Loud Silents: Origins of the Social Problem Film
Looking Far North: The Harriman Expedition to Alaska, 1899 (co-authored with William H. Goetzmann)

Poetry:

The Birds Are On Fire

Miller Williams

As anyone who has ever heard him read knows, Miller Williams is a courtly gentleman deeply committed to his craft as a writer. The same gentle wit, acute observations, and gift for narrative that permeate his poetry are prevalent in his first collection of short stories, *The Lives of Kelvin Fletcher.*

Miller Williams is the author, coauthor, or translator of thirty two books. A University Professor of English and Foreign Languages at the University of Arkansas, his honors include the Prix de Rome for Literature of the American Academy of Arts and Letters, the Academy Award for Literature, and the Amy Lowell Award. Some of America's best-known writers contributed essays to the book *Miller Williams and the Poetry of the Particular*, edited by Michael Burns.

You started your career in the sciences...

I was writing poems and stories from the time I could hold a pencil, and enrolled in college as an English major. In those days, incoming freshmen at most schools were given aptitude tests during the first semester so they could take best advantage of their natural talents. I'd been attending classes for a few weeks when I was called into the office of the head of the psychology department, who said to me in a solemn voice, "Mr. Williams, your tests show that you have no natural ability to use language; if you don't want to embarrass your parents, you need to change you major right away to the hard sciences." I'd been taught to respect authority and learning, so I did as he suggested and continued on that path to what we used to call the AbD (all but dissertation) while I taught biology and chemistry on the college level for twelve years.

I was teaching at Wesleyan College in Macon, Georgia, when Flannery O'Connor—who lived close by and had become a dear friend—contacted Louisiana State University and told them that they ought to talk to me about filling an advertised position for a poet. Preposterous as it must have sounded, they couldn't shrug off a recommendation from her, so they asked to see my work. When they did, they offered me the position. That was in 1962.

When did you become a part of the writing program at Arkansas? Were you one of the founders?

I didn't start the writing program at Arkansas; it was founded by James Whitehead and William Harrison, who asked me to join them in 1971. I founded the translation program, the comparative literature program and—in 1980—the press. I directed it for fifteen years, then returned to the classroom. Whatever I've been doing, I've always reserved the necessary time in the evening for writing.

Many of your poems feel like short stories...

I said to Flannery once, "You call what you're writing stories, but they read to me like long poems." She said, "That's interesting; you call what you write poems, but they seem to me more like short stories."

Is Kelvin Fletcher an alter-ego? Did you set out to write a "coming of age" story?

Some of Kelvin's adventures were mine, some were events in the lives of my friends, and some began with "What if...?" This is true in the case of any fiction writer, I think.

No, I can't say that I intended to write any sort of story; I start the character on his way and follow him, writing down what I see and hear.

You've published in several genres—poetry, translation, and fiction; have you noticed any differences in the way the books are promoted?

I've never felt that there was a difference in the marketing of the various genre. What's important is familiarity with the publishers—of journals or books—and submitting one's work to a publisher who seems inclined to publish the sort of work one does. This is what I try to get across to my students.

You were born in Hoxie, Arkansas. What are some of the changes in the region during your lifetime?

I was born in Hoxie in 1930, but as my father was a Methodist minister—all of whom were itinerant at the time—we moved every two-to-four years. By the time I graduated from high school in Fort Smith in 1947, I'd lived all over the northern half of the state. I did, of course, grow up around fundamentalist conservatives, and they do populate some of my work, but they didn't include my parents, who were integrationist populists; my father was co-founder of the Southern Tenant Farmers' Union, America's first integrated union.

The changes in the South during my lifetime have been more than gratifying to me. George Haley, one of the first black students in the University of Arkansas law school, is my spiritual brother—we call ourselves brothers—and we like to think that we helped some of those changes along, years ago. He's godfather of my daughter Lucinda.

Members of your family often have cameos in your work...

I couldn't talk seriously about my life or my writing without bringing them in. My parents, my five siblings, the three children, the grandchildren, and the great-grandchildren are an essential part of whatever I am and do. This is not to mention Jordan, my wife, who makes me possible.

What's your next project?

I have a collection of essays about poetry and the people who write it coming out from the Louisiana State University Press, and I'm working on a collection of poems, and a college-level textbook on the form and theory of poetry.

Who were your mentors?

I've been extremely fortunate in the attention turned to me and my work by my elders. After Flannery, those who've thought it was worthwhile to turn me in a new direction, put in a word for me somewhere, or simply to read my work and tell me what needed to be done to it, have been Robert Frost, John Crowe Ransom, Elizabeth Bishop, Kenneth Patchen, John Ciardi, Howard Nemerov, John Nims, John Clellon Holmes, Maxine Kumin…Let's just say that I've been greatly blessed.

Selected bibliography Miller Williams

Fiction:

The Lives of Kelvin Fletcher

Poetry:

Some Jazz A While: Collected Poems
The Way We Touch: Poems
A Circle of Stone
So Long at the Fair
The Only World There Is
Halfway from Hoxie
Points of Departure
Adjusting to the Light
Living on the Surface: New and Selected Poems

Critical Works:

Patterns of Poetry: An Encyclopedia of Form

Jan Willis

Despite having left Alabama three decades ago Jan Willis still thinks of Birmingham as "home." When the winters in Connecticut are harsh, she smiles and asks herself, "How did I get stuck up here?" In her memoir, the author and editor of six previous academic books on Buddhism turns inward writing about the wounds of race and the healing process of envisioning positive human emotions. When Willis, who has been writing since high school finally "stopped denying" that she yearned to be a "writer," everything worked in a neat circle to publish and promote *Dreaming Me*. First published in April 2001 as *Dreaming Me: An African-American Woman's Spiritual Journey*, the book was published as a trade paperback as *Dreaming Me: From Baptist to Buddhist; One Woman's Spiritual Journey*.

Do you see *Dreaming Me* as being a part the Southern literary tradition, the spiritual literary tradition, or the non-fiction prose tradition?

All three traditions! My family knew Alex Haley and the book was certainly influenced by *Roots* as well as the African-American literary traditions, and slave narratives.

Eudora Welty is my favorite writer. She uses rich details and what an eye she had. I followed her practice of reading the chapters of the book aloud with a good friend sitting on the sofa listening to the language and details.

The book follows spiritual traditions. I have received NEH fellowships and had been taught to write in a ritualistic way by Tibetan teachers. When I was approached about writing a trade book, I said, "No, I am an academic writer." My students kept writing on my evaluations, "She tells a good story." I had been writing since I was in elementary school and always wanted to write. I had been asked to write this family history and had been working on it. Everything clicked and moved in a neat circle to produce the book.

How did your parents influence *Dreaming Me?*

My mother was a storyteller. She worried about my soul, pushing me toward the church while my father urged us to think for ourselves. He was a self-educated orator. He would raise questions helping to get my mind turning.

What, if any, responses have you received from Southern readers?

I know some people in the South have read and enjoyed *Dreaming Me*. I've gotten lots of emails telling me how much the book has been appreciated, mirrored life, etc. It's really been very gratifying. (I've also gotten thank you emails from Tibetan monks in India and from Black South African Buddhists.)

How can new readers find your earlier books?

Only Enlightened Beings and *Feminine Ground*—besides *Dreaming Me*—are in print and easily accessible. My two earlier books, *The Diamond Light; An Introduction to Tibetan Buddhist Meditation* (1972), and *On Knowing Reality: (a translation and commentary on) The Tattvartha Chapter of Asanga's Bodhisattvabhumi* (1979; reprinted in India), are harder to find, but still do-able. After libraries, I generally advise people to go to the net, for example, amazon.com.

Do you have any recommendations for the spiritual seeker?

Count your blessings. Imagine yourself in another person's shoes. Learn to do that before looking for a group. Visit different places to find a supportive community. Talk with students. You can learn what you need to know from talking with students.

What is your next writing project?

I am currently enjoying very much conducting a series of workshops on practical meditations and exercises for increasing self-esteem at the York Correctional Institute for Women (Connecticut's only women's prison). I do the workshops together with my good friend, Marlies Bosch, a Dutch woman with lots of experiences leading workshops in the Netherlands and with whom I am co-authoring a book entitled, *Transforming Prejudice: Practical Exercises and Meditations.* That's the next book.

Would you like to talk about *Transforming Prejudice?*

The publication of *Dreaming Me* opened up the opportunity to work at York and the experience has been transformative for us as well as the women inmates.

In the workshop we discuss the immense difficulties of putting into practice the Judeo-Christian injunction to "Love one's neighbor as thyself." In our Transforming Prejudice Workshops, we moved methodically through the dismantling of harmful prejudices, beginning with the recognition that we all harbor them...For a future of peace to be possible, we must find methods for disarming our own hearts, ridding them of hateful stereotypes about others and of self-loathing and limiting views of ourselves.

When you started writing *Dreaming Me,* it was your intention to write about your family genealogy, do you plan to return to that project?

Next academic year I'll be on sabbatical and will then finally get the chance to return to my family history work. This is where my passion was when I was asked to write the memoir. I'm looking forward to getting back to that research and the book I'm writing about the roller-coaster emotional process of doing such research. It's called *My Search for Kin.* I've located seven of the eights in line of "great-great grands." I didn't try to follow the line all the way back to Africa.

Do you have any insights to the emotional state of America post 9/11?

The emotional state of America? Fear is a frightening and a terrible thing. Terror is meant to paralyze us; hence to fight it, we must continue to act—to think and to feel. Now is the time to seriously reflect upon prejudice and hatred and see if we can get to the roots of those negative emotions. I worry that the new wave of patriotism may be only a temporary coming together; an 'us' against 'them' thing. Of course, it would be wonderful if the world and its nation-states would, as a result of the all-out assault against terrorism, completely disarm themselves, but that seems an unlikely scenario. What we can and must do, I think, is begin with ourselves, first by disarming our own hearts, then by looking deeply into the causes of hatred, and then by seeking to build bridges.

Selected bibliography Jan Willis

Non-fiction:

Dreaming Me: An African American Womans's Spiritual Journey
Enlightened Beings: Life Stories from the Ganden Oral Tradition
The Diamond Light: An Introduction to Tibetan Buddhist Meditation

Pam Kingsbury, a member of both the National and Southern Book Critics Circle, is a regular book reviewer for *Library Journal, ForeWord, FirstDraft,* and *Southern Scribe*. Her work has also appeared in *America, BookPage,* and several Alabama newspapers. She earned her MA in Creative Writing at the University of New Mexico in Albuquerque and currently teaches in the English Department at the University of North Alabama in her hometown of Florence, Alabama.